ARCHAEOLOGICAL THEORY
THE BASICS

Archaeological Theory: The Basics is an accessible introduction to an indispensable part of what archaeologists do. The book guides the reader to an understanding of what theory is, how it works and the range of theories used in archaeology.

The growth of theory and the adoption of theories drawn from both the natural and social sciences have broadened our ability to produce trustworthy knowledge about the past. This book helps readers to see the value of archaeological theory and beyond what is sometimes thought to be just the use of indigestible jargon. Key theories and concepts are introduced to the reader. Among the main questions discussed are the following:

- What is theory and why do we need it?
- Which major areas of theory are, and have been, used and debated in archaeology?
- What do they tell us about themes including human society, evolution, culture, identity and agency?
- How might archaeological theory change in the future?

This book is written mainly for readers new to archaeology and will help them to understand archaeological theory. It assumes no prior knowledge of archaeological theory and presents it in a selective and clear way, with case studies showing how theory is used in practice.

Robert Chapman is Emeritus Professor of Archaeology at the University of Reading. His research interests include the later prehistory of Iberia, the development of inequalities in human societies, and archaeological theory.

The Basics Series

The Basics is a highly successful series of accessible guidebooks which provide an overview of the fundamental principles of a subject area in a jargon-free and undaunting format.

Intended for students approaching a subject for the first time, the books both introduce the essentials of a subject and provide an ideal springboard for further study. With over 50 titles spanning subjects from artificial intelligence (AI) to women's studies, *The Basics* are an ideal starting point for students seeking to understand a subject area.

Each text comes with recommendations for further study and gradually introduces the complexities and nuances within a subject.

INFANCY
Marc H. Bornstein and Martha E. Arterberry

EDUCATIONAL NEUROSCIENCE
Cathy Rogers and Michael S. C. Thomas

CLASSICAL MYTHOLOGY (SECOND EDITION)
Richard Martin

PLAY DIRECTING: THE BASICS
Damon Kiely

ARCHAEOLOGICAL THEORY: THE BASICS
Robert Chapman

For more information about this series, please visit: www.routledge.com/Routledge-The-Basics-Series/book-series/TBS

ARCHAEOLOGICAL THEORY

THE BASICS

Robert Chapman

LONDON AND NEW YORK

Cover image: Bronze Age rock art, Ormaig, Scotland, Andrew Cochrane & Aaron Watson

First published 2023
by Routledge
4 Park Square, Milton Park, Abingdon, Oxon OX14 4RN

and by Routledge
605 Third Avenue, New York, NY 10158

Routledge is an imprint of the Taylor & Francis Group, an informa business

British Library Cataloguing-in-Publication Data
A catalogue record for this book is available from the British Library

ISBN: 978-1-138-10124-1 (hbk)
ISBN: 978-1-138-10123-4 (pbk)
ISBN: 978-1-315-65709-7 (ebk)

DOI: 10.4324/9781315657097

Typeset in Bembo Std
by codeMantra

CONTENTS

FIGURES AND TABLES

FIGURE

TABLES

BOXES

PREFACE

Anyone who has read archaeological publications will have come across the word 'theory', along with its own (often polysyllabic) vocabulary drawn from disciplines in the natural and social sciences. The introduction of such concepts and ideas from other disciplines was greeted with horror and indignation by many established archaeologists in the 1960s. Five decades later, theory is recognised as being as essential as practice for an education in, and understanding of, archaeology. But there is still a suspicion that basic ideas are being hidden behind a wall of jargon. For example (and I am not picking on the writer), take the claim that Neolithic burial cairns on Orkney 'provided externalized ontological security within a fluid and transient regime of dwelling'.

This book is intended for anyone interested in archaeology as a hobby or career, or beginning to study archaeology on a degree course, or perhaps already participating in field archaeology but still more than a little baffled by theory. I hope to persuade the reader that theory is embedded in the 'doing' of archaeology, essential to our understandings of the past, as well as being intellectually stimulating. It does not have to be confusing: once defined and set into context, initially daunting ideas and concepts become more familiar. I try to define key concepts, introduce the main theories and schools of thought and show the diversity of theoretical approaches, as well as their strengths and weaknesses. Selective coverage is unavoidable given the sheer volume of the literature on theory and the word limit of this book. Theories also vary in popularity at any one time, but it is important that we understand their nature and history when we encounter their use in articles and books, whenever these were published.

There are several books that are used as texts on archaeological theory (e.g. Hodder and Hutson 2003; Praetzellis 2015; Harris and Cipolla 2017; Urban and Schortman 2019; Johnson 2020). These vary in their detail, their scope, the emphasis they give to different theories and their accessibility to readers new to the subject matter. More thematic studies of theoretical issues are presented in edited volumes and readers (e.g. Preucel and Hodder 1996; Thomas 2000; Hodder 2012a). All texts on theory in archaeology are written from the particular standpoint, education and experience of the author(s), whether in relation to specific theories or the ways in which we use our data to produce knowledge of the human past. This book is no different, but I have tried to be as balanced as I can in my presentation and assessment of different theories. For the reader's benefit, I raise questions and criticisms and try to show a diversity of theories in archaeological use. Shaded boxes give more detail on interesting ideas or case studies. References cited in the text are in the English language, although I also include some examples of theory from non-English-speaking regions and countries. It is important to accept that archaeological theory is not the exclusive contribution of the Anglo-American world. The end of each chapter contains suggestions for further reading. Key theories and concepts are highlighted in bold where they are introduced in the text.

ACKNOWLEDGEMENTS

I am indebted to Matt Gibbons at Routledge for the invitation to write this book and for his patience and encouragement during its preparation. Richard Bradley, Rob Hosfield, Matthew Spriggs and Bruce Routledge read draft chapters and offered helpful comments on their contents. Sarah Lambert-Gates prepared Figure 4.1. Jo Brück, Rachel Crellin, Alfredo González-Ruibal, Gavin Lucas, Lynn Meskell and John Robb responded constructively, and at short notice, to a request for their thoughts on the immediate future of archaeological theory. Their responses were very helpful in the structure and content of Chapter 6, although the selection of topics was ultimately my own. Thank you all.

WHAT IS THEORY AND WHY DO WE NEED IT?

What is archaeology? What do archaeologists do? Ask these questions to anyone where you live, work or study, and you will hear about excavation, the digging up of ancient material remains, rich burials and scientific methods of analysis. Fieldwork and laboratory studies dominate the popular image of archaeology. Whether you are beginning an archaeology degree course, or are driven by curiosity, your expectations will be of a practical subject that will give you opportunities for exercise, imagination, team work, a sun tan and above all the opportunity to learn at first-hand about our past. Archaeological evidence may often be fragmentary and poorly preserved, the discarded and decayed material remains of the lives of our ancestors, but that evidence is used to study important historical topics, from the emergence of the earliest humans, through the use of language, and the development of civilisations and empires, to the history and workings of capitalism. Material remains of the past take us into different worlds, partly through their discovery and study, but also through interpretation, the creative and critical use of our imaginations in turning our data into evidence for our historic and prehistoric pasts.

BEYOND THE WHO, WHAT, WHERE AND WHEN

The nature of archaeological evidence can often elicit scepticism about our ability to answer more than 'who', 'what', 'where' and 'when' questions about our past. Among the leading sceptics are anthropologists, who by tradition live amongst the people they are studying, observing their everyday activities and personal interactions, and historians, who immerse themselves in the written

DOI: 10.4324/9781315657097-1

records of past people and events. The archaeologists' potsherds, stone tools and postholes may seem pretty small beer in comparison with the observation of real people, or the reading of their thoughts and intentions. Scepticism has also extended to those archaeologists who stress the limitations of our evidence and our abilities to talk with any confidence about the daily lives, thoughts and actions of our human ancestors from past centuries and millennia. How can we get beyond saying that in a particular time and place, humans did particular things? How did our ancestors develop language, adopt agriculture or form states and empires? Basically, how do we interpret our data with any confidence or ambition, and how can we ask questions that are of more than parochial significance?

The analogy of the jigsaw puzzle to describe the process of archaeological interpretation is simple and simplistic: we take all the pieces from the box, fit them together and 'discover' the picture (although this is not a true discovery as the picture is on the lid). As archaeologists, we never have all the pieces, and there is more than one possible picture! Any experience of archaeology will make you realise that there are always different pictures/interpretations of the same evidence. Competing interpretations for the adoption of agriculture some 10,000 years ago range from environmental stress to social competition. Interpretations of the decline of empires may range from the actions of leaders or large-scale processes of social, political and economic change.

But surely all we need to do is use our commonsense to decide between different interpretations? A layer of ash and charcoal mixed in with collapsed timber roofing may suggest that a fire destroyed an individual structure or even a whole settlement. But was that fire intentional or accidental? If it was intentional, was it the outcome of warfare or for some other reason (e.g. ritual destruction on abandonment)? We might prefer the inference of warfare because there are many good examples of this practice in the present day. But other possibilities require some kind of evaluation. To take another example, does the presence in a grave of objects made out of precious metals automatically imply that the interred individual was a 'chief', or 'king' or of 'high status'/'prestige'? In both cases, it would be very easy to argue that, using our commonsense, the practices with which we are more familiar in our own culture and lifetime are the most convincing. But are they? Arguments of such 'commonsense' are usually based on assumptions about a common human nature (Box 1.1).

If commonsense interpretations are ethnocentric and require critical evaluation, then perhaps we should turn to a practice that goes back to the origins of both anthropology and archaeology, namely the use of **ethnographic analogies** from present-day, non-Western, indigenous societies (Gamble 2015: 106–7).

BOX 1.1 HUMAN NATURE AND ESSENTIALISM

The idea that all humans share a distinctive 'nature' or 'essence' (**essentialism**) is seen prominently in the writings of Aristotle and Enlightenment political theorists such as Thomas Hobbes, who viewed humans as competitive individuals who needed to be controlled by a centralised state (a pessimistic and fixed view of human nature, justifying the existence of both the state and the monarchy as institutions). Eighteenth-century Enlightenment philosophers argued that there was a natural desire among individuals to improve the conditions of their lives (right-wing politicians might now call it 'aspiration'), driven by characteristics such as ambition and greed. In contrast, Jean-Jacques Rousseau was instrumental in opening 'the door to the suggestion that human nature is in fact historically variable', given the structure of societies at different times (Callinicos 2007: 26). This was a line of thought developed most famously by Karl Marx (1969(1844)), who presented a distinction between 'human nature in general', which had capacities (e.g. language, tool-using, cooperation, intentionality, self-consciousness) and needs (e.g. food, shelter, water) and 'human nature as modified in each historical epoch' (Fromm 1969: 25). This line of argument counters assumptions that all humans, by nature, are competitive and desire wealth, power and prestige. These characteristics are not necessarily hard-wired into humans (i.e. a biological drive). They could equally well be the outcome of the kinds of society in which we have been educated and live, and the values that are at the basis of that society, or our class, ethnicity or gender. Individual competition and desire for wealth, power and prestige are positively valued and pursued in capitalist societies, and we are being ethnocentric in assuming that they are characteristics of all human societies. The worst examples of essentialism are those that justify all kinds of social, political and economic inequalities as the outcome of human nature (for a recent discussion on human nature, see Marks 2009).

In its early days, the observational detail of fieldwork studies (ethnographies) undertaken by anthropologists (and before them the accounts of travellers and missionaries) in the non-Western world was used to put flesh on the bones of archaeological studies of hunter-gatherer and agricultural societies in the Western world (e.g. for the aspects of hunter-gatherer societies such as taboos and rituals that do not 'survive' for archaeological study). Cross-cultural regularities in the behaviour of these societies (e.g. women always made the pottery, men made stone tools) were also sought in ethnography and put to use in archaeology. But these practices often denied the histories of non-Western societies, as well as making a fatal assumption: if analogies for all human behaviour were to be found in ethnography, then archaeology would become superfluous to our study and understanding of past human societies. Or, as two of my Spanish friends put it more strongly, this use of ethnographic models is 'an implicit confession of incompetence by archaeologists' (Lull and Micó 2011: 213).

If the analogy of the jigsaw puzzle does not do justice to the nature of archaeological evidence, appeals to commonsense interpretations are ethnocentric and essentialist, and ethnographic analogies risk assumptions that are racist and ahistorical, how does archaeological interpretation proceed?

LEARNING TO SEE: THE BEGINNINGS OF INTERPRETATION

None of us would claim that archaeological evidence speaks to us, that its meaning is self-evident. From the very beginning of an excavation, we give meaning to what we find. A layer we excavate may be a 'destruction level', another is a 'floor', some features are 'storage pits' or 'rubbish pits' or 'postholes'. Among artefacts, a bell-shaped pot is called a 'beaker', and a bifacially flaked stone tool is a 'hand-axe'. Observation is combined with interpretation in the process of excavation. As Phillip Barker puts it, 'it is virtually impossible to exclude all interpretation, explicit or implicit, from a description of the features, layers and their relationships – the very use of words such as post-hole, floor or hearth implies a considerable degree of interpretation' (1977: 233).

The meanings we give to the features and materials we excavate are not arbitrary but are based on reasoned argument. Programmes of experimental construction and destruction of timber buildings, or observation of how their plans can be recognised after the timbers have decayed, enable us to identify their remains or traces in the ground. The distinction between rubbish pits and storage pits depends on their forms, dimensions and contents, although this may be complicated by the reuse of storage pits for the deposition of rubbish (Box 1.2). The attribution of potsherds or flint artefacts to particular types depends on existing and accepted classifications, often supported by analysis of raw materials, contents and traces

---

BOX 1.2 MEDIEVAL 'RUBBISH' PITS

Following standard practice, the archaeologists of the 1988–89 Deansway excavations of Winchester interpreted the medieval pits they found as examples of three types: cess pits, industrial pits or rubbish pits (Buteux and Jackson 2000). This interpretation was based on the shape and contents of the pits. The expectation was that 'rubbish pits' were domestic in function and contained refuse that was deposited directly or from a midden deposit. The pottery in such pits was expected to include large parts of individual vessels, little worn and contemporary (there was little residual material), and a significant concentration of discrete pottery groups (also indicating contemporary use). To the excavators' surprise, only one pit (1%) of those on Site 2 at Deansway fitted these criteria, and this pit and its contents were interpreted as the outcome of a house fire rather than 'normal' rubbish disposal. As the excavators put it 'either our model of the characteristics of the fill of a rubbish pit is misguided, or the pits are not rubbish pits' (Buteux and Jackson 2000: 194). But if the pits were not used for contemporary disposal of rubbish, what were they used for? Suggestions included drainage sumps, and quarry pits for sand and gravel, or for soil to seal the cesspits or to make earth floors. Whatever the initial function, the pit fillings 'are likely to have derived from material scraped up from the site or excavated from a recently dug pit' (2000: 196). At the very least this suggests that pits that had a primary function of receiving contemporary refuse from particular houses were not as frequent as normally thought by medieval archaeologists.

of use-wear. Smaller potsherds may pose interesting challenges for their interpretation as fragments of particular forms of pottery. The processes of observation, recording and analysis contain 'doubts and uncertainties', with ambiguities in the definition and interpretation of features (Barker 1977: 233) and materials.

Interpretation during excavation draws upon the training and experience of the excavators, their comparative knowledge of types and structures of sites (e.g. houses, churches, villas, forts) and the range of materials found in sites of the same date. Barker's archaeology was extensively grounded in the history of area excavations of prehistoric and medieval timber buildings and their interpretation in northwest Europe and Scandinavia from the 1930s to the 1950s. He was quite explicit in his advocacy of the importance of detailed knowledge of the architecture of standing buildings, their forms and construction methods, as well as the evidence for their destruction, in order to be able to interpret the sometimes highly ephemeral archaeological remains of timber and stone structures (Barker 1977: 112).

Interpretation also involves the archaeologist's use of his/her senses to see colour differences with the naked eye and to feel texture differences when defining and excavating features in different subsoils. This can lead to archaeologists seeing what they expect to see, and sometimes missing what they are not expecting to see. In the case of later prehistoric timber buildings in the British Isles, it took the import of larger-scale excavation methods from continental Europe in the late 1930s (at the Iron Age site of Little Woodbury) to overcome the failure to recognise post-built structures and to consign to history the 'pit dwellings' that had been 'seen' by excavators since the mid-nineteenth century. A similar transformation in powers of 'seeing' timber buildings happened in medieval archaeology in Britain (most famously at the sites of Wharram Percy and Yeavering) after WWII (see discussion and references in Chapman and Wylie 2016: 62–7).

Ian Hodder's (1997) much-cited aphorism that archaeological interpretation occurs 'at the trowel's edge' concisely summarises the processes by which archaeologists' collection and interpretation of the raw data of excavations do not separate observation and interpretation as mutually exclusive and successive activities. Theory and practice are inevitably intertwined.

WHAT IS THEORY AND WHY DO WE NEED IT?

In everyday speech, we use the word 'theory' to signify an idea. Such ideas are speculative and require some kind of evaluation that confronts them with relevant and well-founded evidence, unless we think that we live in a 'post-truth' world in which we choose 'alternative' facts to justify our theories. For some, a 'theory' may be vague and less reliable than 'solid facts'. A good example of this view is the policeman in Conan Doyle's *The Sign of Four*, who refers to 'Mr. Sherlock Holmes, the theorist': theory is for amateurs (Holmes); practice is for professionals (policemen).

But, as we have already seen, 'facts' are given meaning through interpretation from their moment of discovery; they are '**theory-laden**'. The opposition between theory and practice is a false one: the British philosopher and archaeologist Robin Collingwood (1939) argued that their relationship was one of 'intimate and mutual dependence'. Theory is not 'a form of research-free armchair thinking, but the guiding compass of empirical investigation' (Therborn 2010 129). Unfortunately, the discipline of archaeology is largely structured institutionally in the UK and North America to loosen the bonds between theory and practice (see Chapter 6).

We use theory to structure and interpret archaeological evidence. Bruce Trigger (2006: 30–5) presents three different levels (high, middle and low) of theory used in archaeology. All are forms of generalisation. For example, low-level theories are concerned with patterns in archaeological data, organising this data into types, cultures, sequences and patterns of association. As Trigger (2006: 32) puts it, 'these empirical observations never provide explanations but constitute patterns that require explanation' (in the case of 'cultures', that explanation in the first half of the twentieth century took the form of the representation of different groups of people in time and space).

It is middle- and high-level theories that 'propose mechanisms that account for why things are as they are and change as they do in multiple instances' (Trigger 2006: 30–1). But what is the difference between these two levels? The answer to this question has been confused by two uses of the term '**middle-range theory**'. The original use of the term was in the work of the sociologist Robert Merton (see discussion in Raab and Goodyear 1984), who argued that theories were at different levels of generality. Let us take Marxism as an example (see Chapter 2): at its most general level it is a materialist theory of class exploitation based on control of the means of production, but in order to work with the theory in studying our data we need to understand how concepts such as production, class or property are evident in our everyday social practices. This more specific type of theory is what Merton meant by middle-range theory. When the term was introduced into archaeology, there was no mention of this sociological meaning: the archaeological focus was, and remains, on developing an understanding of how the material traces of past societies were formed and transformed through their deposition in what was called the 'archaeological record' (see below). Thus, Binford (1977) distinguished his 'middle-range theory' from what he called 'general theory' (= high-level theory + Merton's middle-range theory).

High-level theories (which are the main focus of this book) are, quite simply, structured bodies of thought that try to answer how and why questions and to make sense of empirical observations. For example, Charles Darwin proposed concepts and processes (adaptation, variation, natural selection) that to this day produce the basis of a well-founded theory of evolution for animal species, while Karl Marx performed a similar exercise (using concepts such as the forces and relations of production) for the study of change in human societies. High- and middle-level theories were little discussed and implicit in archaeology before the 1960s (see below), but the low-level generalisations were part of archaeological practice from the foundations of archaeology in the nineteenth century.

High-level theories, as we shall see, are often a challenging read because of their abstract and specialised concepts. They have also experienced cycles of popularity (Kristiansen 2009: 24–5) as well as periods when they 'collide head on' (Layton 1997: 3). They have their own concepts and traditions; they play a part in determining the questions we ask and the methodologies we use in our practice. As they 'attempt to interrelate concepts about human behaviour rather than to account for specific observations, they cannot be confirmed or falsified directly' but 'their credibility can…be influenced by the repeated success or failure of middle-level theories that are logically dependent on them' (Trigger 2006: 34).

Whether used well (i.e. not just a wall of jargon) or not, theory is indispensable to the interpretation of archaeological evidence.

There are four reasons for this need (cf. Johnson 2020: 3–6). First, archaeologists need to construct interpretations that are coherent and make sense of the available evidence, or that are at least more coherent and make more sense than alternative interpretations. Second, if theory permeates archaeological practice and is one of the bases of archaeological interpretation, we need to be as explicit as possible about the theories we are using and their strengths and weaknesses. Third, an explicit use of high-level theories enables us to channel our research, ask new questions and collect new data. Fourth, we need to be explicit about our own social, economic and political standpoints and backgrounds and how they influence our choice of problems to study, theories to use and interpretations to construct (Box 1.3).

BOX 1.3 AN ARCHAEOLOGIST AND HER ARCHAEOLOGY

If archaeology were a detached, objective discipline in which our observations led directly and uncontentiously to our interpretations, there would be little need to know about the archaeologists. But interpretation is a complex and subtle practice to which individual archaeologists bring their own characteristics and experiences: they have class backgrounds, education and values that influence the problems they think worthy of study in the past, as well as their choice of theories to use. Notice the word 'influence' rather than 'determine'. Their interpretations can still be wrong, or less convincing than others, given the archaeological evidence. But their backgrounds, their archaeological training and the professional and institutional networks to which they belong are instructive in any understanding of how they practice archaeology (e.g. the accounts given in Rathje *et al.* 2013).

Let us take an example: John Chapman (1998) outlines some links between the personal and professional life of Marija Gimbutas (1921–4), a renowned specialist in the study of the Neolithic and Bronze Age archaeology of Eastern and Central Europe. Her most famous interpretation contrasted the peaceful, egalitarian, goddess-worshipping agriculturalists of Neolithic 'Old European Culture', with the warlike, more hierarchical and male-dominated, pastoral invaders of the 'Kurgan culture'. What were seen as marked changes in the archaeological evidence between these two cultures were interpreted in terms of the invasion and migration of a different people. Was this an objective interpretation in which the archaeologist's life and experiences played no part? Chapman argues that Gimbutas' gender (and its challenges for her career development) coupled with her shattering experience of modern invasions (successive Russian and German ones of her native Lithuania in the early 1940s) played an important role in her view of cultural change in Eastern and Central Europe. Women were given a more central role in Old European culture, as seen in the goddess worship symbolised in Neolithic figurines, as opposed to the later, male-dominated Kurgan culture. The concept of an Old European culture was inspired by Gimbutas' idyllic youth in the strongly traditional Lithuania, while the Kurgan culture symbolised 'the loss of that paradise in the most violent form imaginable to an adolescent of such obvious sensitivity' (Chapman 1998: 307). The Kurgan invasion routes into southeast Europe were even comparable to those of the Russians in 1944 (1998: figs. 14.3(A) and 14.3(B)). Gimbutas' interpretations can still be evaluated by the ways in which they used different categories of archaeological evidence, but her choice of interpretations cannot be understood without taking into account her personal biography.

ISMS, THEIR ORIGINS AND BORROWING

The high-level theories used by archaeologists to construct interpretations of the human past are not archaeological in origin. Instead, they are appropriated from the social, historical and biological sciences (as are a variety of analytical methods). During the last six decades, archaeologists have behaved like predators in their pursuit and consumption of theories. I have already mentioned Marxism and Darwinism, but other prominent theories that have been 'hunted' by archaeologists include structuralism, feminism, optimal foraging theory, phenomenology, structuration theory and systems theory. The addition of the prefix 'post', as in postcolonialism or poststructuralism, is used to make clear when the original theory is argued to be in need of radical transformation or discard.

The borrowing of theories can be both challenging and divisive. New and strange concepts are introduced, often to the bafflement of archaeologists who have only just become accustomed to reading about, and using, the existing range of theories. It may not be immediately clear how the new theories can help us to do archaeology, given the nature of our evidence and practice. We may also not understand the contexts in which new theories have been developed, given that we are archaeologists and not anthropologists, sociologists or philosophers. Some new high-level theories have a comparatively short popularity in archaeology, while others become incorporated into the mainstream. For every archaeologist whose palate is broadened by the consumption of new theories, there are others who find them indigestible.

Archaeological debate over theories has become 'very abstract and specialized' (Hodder 2012b: 2), especially in the diverse range of concepts, ideas and language that are used and the conferences and publication outlets in which 'theorists' present and discuss their ideas. As a result, this debate is 'rarified and removed' (2012b: 5) from the experience of everyday practitioners in the field. Debate in the 1960s was between those who did or did not advocate the importance of explicit theory, a relatively simple division into two camps. The papers and books on archaeological theory were relatively small in number and it was easy to develop a clear picture of contending positions and arguments. The following five decades have seen a fragmentation into so many theoretical camps that are not necessarily mutually intelligible: this fragmentation and the pace of publication make it almost impossible to keep up with new theories and theoretical debate.

The very nature of these high-level theories is that they are not unified bodies of thought (hence the old joke about one Marxist being able to start a fight in an empty room); internal diversity and conflict gives them a mechanism for change. No one theory will hold the answer to the interpretation of the world around us (what is called '**underdetermination')**, and different theories direct us to different questions: for example, the nature, amount, scale and degree of preservation of archaeological evidence for the 'fall' of the Roman Empire may be more productively studied by the application of multiple theories than by the exclusive pursuit of one. Archaeology cannot necessarily be divided neatly into practitioners who agree on their understanding of particular theories, or who slavishly follow only one body of theory throughout their careers. They may adopt new theories that are thought to be more coherent and convincing than the old ones, or that enable them to make better sense of their evidence. There are also examples of 'pick-"n"-mix' approaches, drawing on different theories in a more pluralistic way.

THREE TYPES OF ARCHAEOLOGY

Read any book on archaeological theory, especially in the Anglo-American world, and you will soon be confronted by a division into three successive types, namely 'traditional' (up to the 1960s), 'processual' (initially called 'new archaeology', 1960s–70s) and 'postprocessual' (emerging at the end of the 1970s). I have used the word 'types', although processual and postprocessual archaeologies could be called 'schools' (at least, in their formative days in Chicago and Cambridge respectively), 'paradigms' (a term introduced with the new/processual archaeology but losing meaning since the 1980s – Lucas 2016) or 'research programmes' (Gibbon 2014: 51). Early processual archaeology in North America was famously compared to a religion, with its spiritual leader (Lewis Binford) and a group of disciples. Whichever word is used, it is important to note that each approach incorporates diversity and debate, and 'any claim for a neat distinction between… (these approaches)…is unsustainable' (Hodder 2012b: 9).

Traditional archaeology was so named by the new/processual archaeologists in the early 1960s and referred to what was seen as the dominant practices and aims of the senior generation in the profession at that time: the collection, description and classification of objects (whether structural or portable); their grouping together in 'cultures' with shared 'norms' (hence **normative**) that represented 'peoples' in the past; the study of similarities and differences between cultures and their regional arrangement in sequences (**culture history**); emphasis on specific histories of specific cultures (**historical particularism**); the use of concepts of migration and diffusion to explain changes in cultures; and a sceptical view of the potential to make inferences about some aspects of past cultures (e.g. social and political organisation) from fragmentary and ephemeral archaeological data (e.g. Hawkes 1954).

Traditional archaeology was criticised for its neglect of theory. While comparatively few archaeologists before the 1960s would have thought of themselves as practising theory, the collection and analysis of archaeological data, the study of 'cultures' and the inferences of diffusion and migration from material evidence required theoretical arguments. For example, what are cultures and how do they change? The archaeologist most associated with culture history in archaeology from the 1920s to the 1950s was Gordon Childe (see Box 2.2), who was also distinguished by his use of Marxist theory to study social evolution. Given the fragmentary nature of archaeological data, ethnographic analogies were used to suggest functional uses of material culture, and the nature of past social relations and subsistence practices (e.g. Clark 1952), while geographical ideas about environment and society drove generalisations about the relationships between landscape and culture change in prehistoric Britain (Fox 1932). These examples suggest that theoretical practice before the 1960s was under the radar, implicit rather than explicit, and markedly underdeveloped. However, there were periodic 'crisis debates' in North America about archaeology's capacity to test hypotheses and explain rather than just describe patterns in its data, and to use theory to articulate practice (Wylie 2002: 25–41). The next type of archaeology can be seen as a development and intensification, and for many (incorrectly) a resolution, of these debates.

New/Processual Archaeology criticised traditional archaeology and was initiated in the work of Lewis Binford (e.g. see papers in Binford and Binford 1968 and Binford 1972) and his students at the University of Chicago. In this approach, scepticism was replaced by optimism about the potential to make inferences about past societies from archaeological data: there were no inherent limitations to our knowledge of the past; rather we had to address what Binford called our 'methodological naivete' (Binford 1968: 23). This optimism enabled, for example, inferences linking pottery design to practices of post-marital residence and membership of descent groups in prehistoric societies (e.g. Deetz 1968). Instead of focusing on particular, historical sequences of cultures, new archaeologists aimed to make generalisations, even laws, about human behaviour and the processes by which culture changes. The use of the singular, 'culture', is important here: rather than 'cultures' as the material representation of specific groups of people, 'culture' has been used in anthropology since the 1870s to indicate learned rather than inherited forms of behaviour (see Chapter 4) and, following the anthropologist Leslie White, Binford viewed 'culture' as a means by which humans adapted to the world around them. A specific culture was studied as a **system**, that is, a functioning whole, with all its parts (society, economy, politics, etc.) interrelated (see Clarke 1968: fig. 23). Archaeologists were charged with trying to explain, not just describe, stability and change in these cultures. This focus on explanation stemmed from an immersion in the scientific method (or at least a specific version of that method) and a requirement that research proceed by the study of specific problems or questions, and the testing of hypotheses against archaeological data. This view of culture put theory up front (**General Theory**), while the making of inferences about past societies required links to be made between archaeological data (e.g. animal bones, artefacts) and past behaviour (Binford's **Middle-Range Theory**). If archaeologists propose the existence of hierarchies in past societies from, for example, distributions of pottery types in and between excavated house structures, that inference can be strengthened by study of the use and discard of pottery in modern, non-Western societies (**ethnoarchaeology**): do such societies use pottery to mark out social distinctions, and do they dispose of it exactly where it has been made and used?

New/processual archaeology was anthropological (rather than historical), explanatory, generalising (about cultural processes), theoretical, scientific in method, and optimistic about the inferences that could be made from archaeological data. It was a dramatic break with 'traditional' archaeology and marked a generational shift in the discipline. It drew upon theories from disciplines such as ecology, cybernetics, anthropology and architecture. But as processual archaeology grew, it diversified, and opinions varied on the extent to which archaeologists could produce laws of human behaviour that were any more than trivial (Flannery 1973 called them 'Mickey Mouse laws'). The forms that new/processual archaeology took in North America and Europe differed over issues such as the application of the 'scientific method' (Clarke 1973), and archaeology's situation within either anthropology or history. Binford himself rejected the pursuit of laws of human behaviour (as advocated in Schiffer 1976) and focused his research on the development of his middle-range theory (e.g. 1978, 1981).

In North America and Europe, the adoption of processual approaches occurred in a context of expanding employment in higher education, but more traditional approaches also continued to be practised by an older generation, and in a field/commercial archaeology that expanded to meet threats to the heritage. The outcome was a polarisation between theory and practice, and between university and field archaeology, especially in the 1970s. Traditional archaeology did not disappear overnight, while new/processual archaeology was not a unified critique and practice: in fact, the debates within it played an important role in its transformation.

According to the usual introductory accounts, this transformation was to **Postprocessual Archaeology** which emerged as a systematic critique of processual archaeology by Ian Hodder and a critical mass of students at Cambridge University (e.g. Hodder 1982a, 1982b, 1986; Shanks and Tilley 1987a, 1987b). The importance of theory, problem orientation and expanding the range of inferences that archaeologists could make about the past continued, along with ethno-archaeological research, but the range of theories expanded (e.g. structuralism, poststructuralism, structuration theory, critical theory) and the complexity of the relationship between human behaviour and material culture was given greater emphasis. A study of the symbolism and meaning of material culture was advocated within the context of historical sequences in the human past, while cross-cultural generalisations and laws of human behaviour were rejected. The motor of change was located within human cultures rather than in their adaptation to the external world, and the actions of individuals were given an important role in this process. The use of the natural sciences as a model for the workings of archaeological interpretation was rejected, and archaeologists were seen as working within social and political contexts (rather than being 'neutral' scientists). Debates with processual archaeology ensued (e.g. compare and contrast Binford 1982 and Hodder 1982c), and a diaspora of Cambridge students occurred (mainly in UK universities) along with publication of case studies and conferences.

Once again, the usual introductory accounts on archaeology and archaeological theory are somewhat oversimplified. Rather than being a simple succession of unified approaches, archaeology was undergoing a diversification as its practitioners explored the range of theories in the social sciences and what the philosophy of science could offer by way of guidance in seeking to understand how to build trustworthy knowledge of the past. Processual archaeology has remained embedded in North America, while a more historical approach to archaeology was disinterred (along with the work of its practitioners in the pre-/post-WWII period) in the UK (e.g. Hodder 1987). There were also examples of boundary crossing as well as the blurring of boundaries as some archaeologists educated in the processual tradition reacted positively to the postprocessual critique. What were initially tightly-knit 'schools' based mainly on individual university departments have become more diversified traditions of thought (e.g. see Hodder 2012b: fig. 1.1) with a developing range of theories and approaches. In North America, Michelle Hegmon (2003: 218) describes the development of a **processual-plus archaeology** that 'takes on postprocessual themes but attempts to develop systematic methodologies and generalizable conclusions'. Among the themes of the postprocessual critique that have been adopted into the 'processual (plus) mainstream' are symbolism and meaning, gender and agency (p. 217), showing 'an openness and dynamism that result from dialogue across theoretical lines' (p. 219) by archaeologists who 'are not excessively attached to or dismissive of any particular approach and seem to be open to multiple ways of viewing the past' (p. 233).

Archaeologists in the Anglo-American world may, or may not, identify themselves with processual or postprocessual approaches as a whole, or may work with particular theories (e.g. evolutionary, Marxist), or may be wary of aligning themselves overtly with a single theoretical approach. Outside this world, the impact of processual and postprocessual archaeologies has been both uneven and selective (e.g. Chapman 2003: 15–26 for a brief survey and references). Here many archaeologists reject the notion that theoretical debate can only be framed within the historical context of dominant, Western traditions of archaeological thought. With justification, we are asked by Mediterranean and Latin American archaeologists what *we* can learn from *their* theoretical approaches and *their* articulation of theory and practice.

WHAT HAS PHILOSOPHY OF SCIENCE DONE FOR US?

All archaeologists, of whatever theoretical persuasion, have had to engage with the philosophy of science since the 1960s, thus providing further '-ologies' and '-isms' to surprise them! Among the questions raised by the philosophy of science are the following: what is the nature of reality? what kinds of concepts do we use to describe that reality in all its forms? what is the nature of knowledge? what are its limits? how do we know what we claim to know? These questions are grouped together into two fields of study: **Ontology** and **Epistemology**.

Mario Bunge (2003: 201) defines ontology as 'the branch of philosophy that studies the most pervasive features of reality, such as real existence, change, time, causation, chance, life, mind and society'. Alison Wylie (in Chapman and Wylie 2016: 46–7, note 4) states that 'ontological questions concern what exists, the nature of being or reality and, by extension, the status of the categories and concepts in terms of which we describe and explain things that we take to exist'. Archaeologists use a variety of 'categories and concepts' to enable them to 'describe and explain' what we think existed in the past: we define types of artefacts (e.g. Beaker pots, Folsom points, Bellarmine jugs), structures (e.g. 'houses', 'ritual') and sites (e.g. 'villages', 'towns', 'villas', 'causewayed enclosures'), and we organise them into successive periods and groupings such as assemblages, stone-tool industries, cultures, political units (e.g. states, empires) and the much-vaunted civilisations. Without these 'categories and concepts' we could not move from our excavated data to grand ideas about human history.

When we have categorised types of objects, structures and sites, the next stage has been to arrange them in time and space. But what are time and space? Are they external dimensions that simply place our finds in relative and absolute sequences (archaeological periods calibrated by absolute dating methods) and at different distances and directions from each other? Or are they concepts that are culturally defined, creating and created by social relations? (see Gamble 2015: 151–84, or Chapter 4).

Also subject to debate is the concept of the **archaeological record**, an inescapable term used in archaeology since at least the mid-1950s, although popularised by Lewis Binford from the late 1960s. What is it? All surviving material traces of the past, above or below ground? Before or after excavation? The matrix of soil and sediments that envelops these material traces of objects and structures? Or as Gavin Lucas (2012: 9) argues, it 'can – and perhaps ought to – entail both the physical remains themselves and the work archaeologists perform on them to constitute them as archaeological evidence'. Is it dead and in the present (e.g. Binford 1977), or alive (think of all the biological and chemical processes active in the ground) and in the present, waiting for archaeologists to find ways of 'reconstructing' what happened in the past, taking us from the observable present to the unobservable past (Schiffer's 1972 division between a systemic context in the past and an archaeological context in the present)?

A series of broader and more tantalising ideas and debates concern the nature of reality, especially the reality of human existence. What is this reality composed of? This is a question that has divided philosophers since Classical times and has two, polarised, answers: **Materialism** holds that 'reality is composed exclusively of material or concrete things' (Bunge 2003: 172) (see also, Chapter 2), while **Idealism** 'asserts the primacy of ideas or even their independent existence' (135). Debates between 'materialists' and 'idealists' are important for archaeologists when they consider such issues as how and why societies changed: did change come about as a result of ideas in the minds of human beings, or as the outcome of change in the material world of human societies? This polarisation of materialist and idealist philosophies is a gross simplification, but it is a starting point.

If that is ontology, then what is epistemology and why do archaeologists need to know about it? Consider the following questions: how do we know what we claim to know about the past? why is one interpretation of the past favoured more than another? how do we evaluate different interpretations? is archaeological reconstruction of past societies an objective or a subjective practice? do our theories determine our interpretations? These questions all raise issues of epistemology, defined by Wylie as focused on 'the nature, limits and scope of knowledge, and the norms of justification by which we establish knowledge claims' (in Chapman and Wylie 2016: 46–7 note 4). Among other things the answers to these questions help us to establish trustworthy claims to knowledge about the human past, in contrast to 'pseudo' archaeologies that claim, for example, transatlantic or extra-terrestrial origins for early American civilisations, lost civilisations covered by modern sea levels, or the construction of the Great Pyramid of Giza in Egypt to produce nuclear energy (for the latter and other examples, see Orser's 2015 well-argued critique).

Epistemological questions and debates have been prominent in the archaeological literature since the 1960s. With some simplification, we may note that the incompleteness of the material traces of our past and its implications for the kinds and depths of knowledge we can gain about it have been issues of discussion in archaeology since the early twentieth century. Going beyond the cataloguing and description of data (what can be seen and touched) was seen by some as dangerously speculative and subjective (by those who espoused **empiricism**), while others advocated the need for theory, moving beyond observable data to unobservable social, economic and political pasts. Early processual archaeologists advocated an optimistic epistemology based on objectivity and the explicit, value-free, testing of hypotheses against archaeological data as a means to explain the past through laws of cultural processes: beginning with hypotheses and testing them against independent data was contrasted with the traditional collection, study and definition of patterning in data as a means of arriving at some kind of understanding of the past. It did not matter where the hypotheses came from, nor the standpoints of individual archaeologists, as long as they were tested against independently collected data. This emphasis on the 'scientific method' as the means for observing and explaining the world around us was derived from what was known in the philosophy of science as **logical positivism** (e.g. Hempel 1966). Not all processual archaeologists shared this faith in a unified scientific method and the pursuit of laws of human behaviour (e.g. Clarke 1973).

Postprocessualists rejected the concept of a unified, scientific method and turned to a tradition (beginning in the late eighteenth century) of Continental Philosophy known as **hermeneutics** and the works of thinkers such as Wilhelm Dilthey and Hans-Georg Gadamer. Rather than pursue the explanations and laws of the natural sciences, hermeneutic approaches sought to gain 'understandings' in the human sciences (for an introduction and archaeological examples, see Hodder 1999: 30–65). The collection and study of data were argued not to be independent of theory, nor of the standpoints of archaeologists and the social and political worlds in which they worked. Archaeology was not the wholly objective practice depicted in processualism.

In more extreme cases, the stress on the social and cultural contexts in which archaeological research was practised led ultimately to the conclusion that 'there is no way of choosing between alternative pasts except on essentially political grounds, in terms of a definite value system, a morality' (Shanks and Tilley 1987b: 195). In other words, the past was constructed in the present and there was no objective way of deciding between our different pasts (although see Hodder 1989), a form of 'extreme' or 'hyper' **relativism** (Trigger 2006: 2–3).

A more moderate relativist position recognises the capacity of our archaeological evidence to constrain our theoretical speculations and confront us with materials, sequences, sites and structural forms that we were not expecting to find. We cannot control the outcomes of research into different lines of evidence, whether these be radiometric dating, isotopic analysis or provenance analysis: each of these methods is based on complex and independent, scientific 'background knowledge', the subject of ongoing assessment by critical communities of non-archaeological researchers (see Chapman and Wylie 2016). This kind of knowledge has also been the focus and outcome of interdisciplinary research on the archaeological record since the 1970s (see middle-range theory, above), aimed at strengthening our inferences of past cultural practices through the specific data at our disposal. We work with multiple methods and multiple lines of evidence (Box 1.4), many beyond our specialist knowledge and requiring collaborative research (we do not do our own radiocarbon dating), and we come to archaeology with a range of theoretical positions and social, political and economic standpoints. But the material traces of the human past can resist 'theoretical appropriation' (Shanks and Tilley 1989: 44). The materials that we study have 'the capacity to surprise, resist, contradict and re-shape knowledge' (Edgeworth 2012: 77). Theory does not determine the outcomes of practice.

BOX 1.4 MULTIPLE LINES OF EVIDENCE: POPULATION MOVEMENT

Population movement is well-documented for the Roman Empire, whether it be on local and regional scales, or spanning much greater distances as a result of military activity. Research on such movement in later Roman Britain has relied heavily on the material evidence provided by the treatment of the dead, especially the nature of their grave goods and any inscriptions present on gravestones. How can this evidence be used to make inferences about the ethnicity of the dead and the nature and scale of population movement? An influential answer to these questions was produced by Clarke (1979), who used the treatment of the dead in the later Roman cemetery at Lankhills in Winchester to infer the presence of 'intrusive' burials representing incomers from the Roman province of Pannonia, roughly what today is western Hungary, eastern Austria and parts of northern parts of the former Yugoslavia. But how reliable are the links made between material evidence and ethnicity? For example, incomers may adopt local material culture and customs while 'locals' may adopt the use of exotic items, especially when those items have a high social value. Given these doubts, it is productive to examine other lines of evidence, in this case the morphological and isotopic analyses of the skeletal remains themselves (Eckardt *et al.* 2009, 2014).

Isotopic analyses on skeletal and dental samples have been developed as measures of population movement: oxygen isotopes characterise the composition of drinking water, and hence the temperature and climate in the area where an individual was born, while strontium isotopes tell us about the geology of the region that provided the food consumed by an individual during his/her lifetime. But similarities in isotopic values between regions of similar climates and geologies require us to use oxygen and strontium analyses as complementary measurements of the likelihood of an individual being 'local' or 'non-local', excluding some regions as areas of origin and establishing consistency with an origin in other areas.

Taking the whole sample of analyses from the Lankhills cemetery, Eckardt *et al.* (2009, 2014) found that about half the individuals were of isotopically 'local' origin, while half came from other regions of Britain, Central/Southern Europe and the Mediterranean. But of the 'local' individuals, about a third were associated with Clarke's 'Pannonian' material culture and burial rites, while five with this mortuary treatment had isotopically 'local' origins. By itself, the treatment of the dead did not predict individual origins, while isotopic analyses did not necessarily match up with either 'local' or 'exotic' grave goods. Reliance on one line of evidence would fail to reveal this more complex picture. There was no simple relationship between mortuary treatment and ethnicity. This invites us to think more critically about the concept of ethnicity and how it is represented alongside other factors such as age, sex and social relations. The isotopic analyses, by themselves, do not provide the 'scientific' answer to the question of origin; they are one line of evidence to be explored alongside the material and osteological lines.

What does this mean for claims that archaeologists are objective students of the human past? The answer to this question does, of course, depend on what is meant by objectivity. But rather than some absolute criterion, whereby objectivity is opposed in a polarised way to subjectivity, the truth lies somewhere in between. Our knowledge claims about our past are 'as robust and reliable as we can make them...they are trustworthy as a basis for further inquiry and for action of various kinds' (Chapman and Wylie 2016: 209). We are not absolutely 'unbiased' and 'detached' from the world as 'value-free' scientists, studying that world from outside it, neither are we speculative 'guessers', without the ability to decide between competing interpretations of the past. Indeed, the different standpoints and perspectives that we bring to archaeology can help us scrutinise existing interpretations and practices, as well as develop new lines of evidence within our discipline. For example, indigenous communities have bodies of knowledge, handed down by oral traditions, about their histories, the ecosystems in which they live and the land management practices on which their subsistence is based. Do we accept these traditions as authentic histories, or only when they are in accord with archaeological research results? In other words, do we give greater weight to science over tradition? Nicholas and Markey (2015) argue that, as archaeologists, we work together with indigenous communities to develop new lines of evidence and questions for study (Chapter 5).

DOES ARCHAEOLOGICAL THEORY EXIST?

This book has the title Archaeological Theory, but given what you have read in this chapter it is not at all unreasonable to ask this question: does specifically *archaeological* theory exist? The main -isms and -ologies and the 'new' and 'post' -isms are either high-level theories (in Trigger's sense), borrowed from the social and biological sciences, or schools/types that have received inspiration and theories from other disciplines. Since the 1960s, archaeology has evolved from a practical discipline that used such theories implicitly or rarely, to one in which theory and practice are both basic to what we do. From our theory borrowing we have learned to think about, and debate, big issues such as the nature of society and social change, the complex relationships between human societies and their environments, the materialisation of social, political and economic differences, the means by which we build and evaluate claims to knowledge about the human past, and the reasons why archaeological knowledge is important in contemporary society. Archaeology has been transformed.

But archaeology is not anthropology, or sociology, or biology or ecology, given that it has unique data, in terms of both its nature and scale (in time and space). Archaeology is not social theory. We cannot observe or talk to our subjects in the past. In this context, it is not surprising that some theories may be more productive for archaeological usage. Clarke (1973) made the point that the theory of archaeological knowledge (see above) cannot simply be borrowed from the physical sciences, but has to be constructed (albeit using philosophical insights) by a critical examination of what archaeologists actually do in practice, working with their distinctive data (see Chapman and Wylie 2016) and evaluating the coherence and correspondence of Trigger's three levels of theory in archaeology. We could call this book 'Theory in Archaeology', but such a title would not do justice to the ways in which archaeologists interpret their data, so Archaeological Theory will suffice.

All theories evolve. Some are more successful than others. They all have their moment in the sun, but they do not all have an equally long period of usage and influence on archaeological interpretation. One theoretical approach that has had a long-standing impact, although not necessarily acknowledged as such and often widely misunderstood, is Marxism. The next chapter will look at the Marxist tradition and try to demonstrate its continuing relevance to archaeology.

SUMMARY

- As archaeologists we study the material traces of past societies, but how we interpret these traces to construct histories is not a simple matter of commonsense or putting together a jigsaw puzzle picture. The data do not speak for themselves and there is no one picture.
- We interpret our data, giving meaning to it, from the moment we start collecting it through activities such as excavation. This interpretation draws on skills learnt through training, experience, comparative knowledge of site types and materials, experimental research, etc.
- Different levels of theory are an essential part of the process of interpretation. In this book, the main focus is on high-level theories drawn from the social and natural sciences.
- Archaeologists disagree, sometimes violently, about the strengths and weaknesses of these theories and of a small number of historical 'schools' or 'research programmes'.
- We have much to learn from the philosophy of science about the concepts we use, the nature of reality and the ways in which we construct knowledge about past human societies.

FURTHER READING

Johnson (2020: 1–12) gives a clear introduction to the nature and need for theory, and in later chapters (2020: 12–121) presents the details and debates of traditional, processual and postprocessual archaeologies. More brief introductions to these, and other, types of archaeology are given by Praetzellis (2015: 9–28), Gamble (2015: 25–56) and Hodder (2012b: 1–14), and in contributions to Renfrew and Bahn (2005). If you want to read a more comprehensive, weighty and larger-scale, international, history of archaeological thought, Trigger (2006) is the best example you will find. The ways in which theory is embedded within archaeological fieldwork are discussed through case studies in Chapman and Wylie (2016: 55–92). Trigger

(2006) will also introduce you to the 'isms' mentioned in the section on philosophy of science. Gibbon (2014) will take you further in thinking about philosophical issues such as explanations of archaeological evidence. Wylie (2002: xi–xv, 1–22) uses her training in, and experience of, both disciplines to present a personal vision of what the philosophy of science can do for archaeology. How archaeologists work with their evidence (whether it be from fieldwork, archives, museum stores, or non-archaeological resources such as radiometric dating and provenance analysis) to build trustworthy interpretations of past human societies is given through case studies in Chapman and Wylie (2016).

2

SOCIAL RELATIONS AND THE LEGACY OF MARX

Social theorists and philosophers since the eighteenth century have posed some ambitious questions about the changing social worlds in which we live. How do social relations shape, and are shaped by, economic and political structures? What is the relationship between individuals and social structures? How do social systems evolve? Are societies balanced, functioning 'wholes' or the battlegrounds for the continuous struggle between classes, or for status, prestige and power? Is there any kind of pattern (e.g. from simple to complex) to the historic development of human societies? More philosophically, are concepts such as progress and rationality helpful in studying changing social worlds?

We could easily devote entire chapters to the work and legacy of three nineteenth-century thinkers, Karl Marx, and the sociologists Max Weber and Emile Durkheim, who are widely regarded as the founding fathers of anthropology. In this chapter, we will focus on the works of Marx and Friedrich Engels, and make some comparison with the ideas of Weber and Durkheim. What did they write, how did it influence subsequent theoretical ideas and what has been their impact on archaeology through to the present day? Introductory texts on archaeology are often brief and selective in their coverage of the high-level theory of Marxism, so a more extensive account is given here.

WHAT DO YOU THINK YOU KNOW ABOUT MARXISM?

What comes into your mind when you hear mention of Marx-ism? Do you associate it with the former communist regimes of Russia and Eastern Europe: totalitarian states that built drab

DOI: 10.4324/9781315657097-2

architecture, repressed their populations, suppressed religious practice and prevented their citizens from having access to the freedoms that are valued in the West? These Stalinist regimes collapsed in the early 1990s, as 'socialism' supposedly lost its political and economic struggle with capitalism. The ideas of Marx and Engels, in the period from the early 1840s to their respective deaths in 1883 and 1895, had been used to legitimise these regimes, but are now claimed by some to be dead and buried.

Is such a view justified? Terry Eagleton (2011) argues that ten of the main objections to the ideas of Marx and Engels are either wrong or fail to do justice to their detailed arguments. In contrast to received wisdom, 'Marx …was a critic of rigid dogma, military terror, political suppression and arbitrary state power … he believed that political representatives should be accountable to their electors … (and) he insisted on free speech and civil liberties' (2011: 21). Stalinist regimes from the 1920s to the early 1990s asserted a doctrinaire, dogmatic and perverted interpretation of the classic works of Marx and Engels that failed to conform to these writers' concept of socialism (Callinicos 1991). In fact, the end of Stalinism provided the opportunity to re-engage freely with the diversity and development of Marxist thought (Callinicos 1999: 12; Hobsbawm 2011: 350). In the words of the geographer David Harvey, it is also time 'to set aside those things that you think you know about Marx so that you can engage with what he actually has to say' (2010: x).

READING MARX AND ENGELS

Reading and understanding the works of Marx and Engels are not straightforward exercises. Some significant works were neither completed nor published during their lifetimes. Engels edited and brought to publication volumes 2–3 of *Capital* after Marx's death. Some manuscripts (e.g. *Pre-capitalist Economic Formations*) were not even intended for publication. English translations of key texts such as *The Economic and Philosophical Manuscripts*, *Pre-capitalist Economic Formations, The German Ideology* and *Grundrisse* were not published until 1959, 1964, 1965 and 1973, respectively. 'For most of the history of Marxism, debate has therefore been based on a varying selection of Marx and Engels' writings' (Hobsbawm 2011: 177). The translation and editing of these works provoke continuing debates over Marx's meaning, and often impede a nuanced, understanding of continuity and change in his thoughts. Given these challenges, I will be selective and highlight key themes and concepts.

MARX AND ENGELS: THE BASICS

The education of Marx and Engels (Berlin 1978; Hunt 2009) brought them into contact with the works of philosophers from Aristotle to Hegel. It is often stated that the key strands of intellectual influence on Marx and Engels were German philosophy, French political theory and English classical economics. In all cases, the works of key thinkers were subjected to incisive critique. Marx wrote as a means to develop his own ideas on a history and critique of industrial capitalism. For all its originality, and unlike Darwin's theory of evolution, this historical and theoretical project did not attract major public attention until the twentieth century. What were some of the key ideas?

BEING HUMAN

As we have seen in Chapter 1 (Box 1.1), Marx argued that humans have capacities and needs, but these are divided into those that are 'general' (e.g. food, clothing, shelter, sleep) and those that are 'historically formed and culturally specific' (e.g. competition) (Geras 1983). Unlike other animal species, humans create new needs and goals in life, as well as change the beliefs, behaviours and attitudes that they value. For example, the position of women in society was not biologically determined, a part of being human, but historically variable (as in the patriarchal society of Victorian England) (Engels 1972).

Human beings are born into natural and social worlds, and their actions maintain and transform these worlds. They use their bodies, perception, consciousness and creativity to conceive and produce the objects needed in their lives. They are natural, social and cultural beings (Patterson 2009: 41–50), but 'their conscious life activity in contrast to that of animals was increasingly determined by social relations and culture' (Patterson 2009: 74). The societies in which humans live are **totalities**: more than the sum of their parts, continually in flux and with a complex web of internal relations.

PRODUCTION AND REPRODUCTION

Human and animal species, no matter what their different capacities, have the need to produce and reproduce. But for humans, production and reproduction are not solely matters of biology (food for consumption, mates for reproduction) but of society and culture (working together to produce things, developing cultural practices to enable both biological and social reproduction). Production requires socially organised human labour, making products of various kinds from raw materials. The combination of physical and mental labour enables humans to transform the worlds in which they live: as archaeologists we see how flint nodules become hand-axes, lumps of clay become pots and trees are cut down to make houses. Human beings work together, using their bodily capacities (e.g. strength, coordination, dexterity) to transform materials into objects to fulfil their needs. Human energy is channelled through what we would call tools, or what Marx and Engels called 'instruments of labour' to make products that are valued for their practical and symbolic use (e.g. what forms and sizes of pots are most useful for particular activities?) and for what they can be exchanged or purchased. As Marx (1969: 95) put it 'the product of labour is labour which has been embodied in an object and turned into a physical thing; this product is an objectification of labour'. Elsewhere he writes that labour is 'materialized …into the form of an object' (1973: 300; for further discussion, see Marx 1972: 1–58). Within the daily life of social groups, time and labour are allocated to all kinds of production. The products are then distributed and consumed by use.

Marx and Engels argue that production consists of two parts (Callinicos 1999: 98ff) (Table 2.1). 'Material' production requires raw materials, instruments of labour and human labour power. Together they make up the **forces of production**. 'Social' production tracks the means by which the process of production and the products themselves are socially organised and controlled (**relations of production**). Are raw materials, tools and products equally accessible to all members of all groups in society, or is such access appropriated by much smaller groups? Nineteenth-century capitalists controlled the **means of production** (in this case, the factory workers, the machinery they used in the factories, the cotton imported from the American south). These means of production were the **property** of

Table 2.1 Forces and relations of production

Forces of production	Social relations of production
Human labour power	Accessibility to, and control of, products, production, distribution and consumption
Raw materials	
Instruments of labour	

the capitalists and their ownership ensured the exploitation of the working class (note this specific use of the word 'property', which should not be confused with an individual's personal possessions).

Different forms of property (e.g. based on institutions such as slavery and feudalism), that is different ways of extracting labour from workers, existed in what Marx called a **mode of production** (e.g. Asiatic, Ancient, Germanic, Feudal and Capitalist). A key concept here was that of surplus labour, defined as 'work undertaken beyond that required to maintain the life of those working and their dependents' (Rosenswig and Cunningham 2017a: 4). Such surplus is present in all societies, but it is organised and consumed in different ways, depending on the social and political structure, and this is central to the reproduction or transformation of society. Marx was particularly interested in the transformation from the feudal to the capitalist mode of production. In feudalism, the serfs were granted land (they owned the means of production) and used their labour in productive and other activities (e.g. giving a proportion of their harvests to their lord) under pressure of physical coercion. In capitalism, the capitalists owned the means of production (e.g. factories, machines), and extracted surplus labour (e.g. by paying less wages to their workers, designing more efficient machinery to increase profits), under pressure of economic coercion. Modes of production are not typologies of societies in fixed orders of development, nor are they mutually exclusive: for example, there could be a dominant mode of production in any one society. The reproduction or transformation of modes of production is studied in particular historical contexts.

A MATERIALIST CONCEPTION OF HISTORY

But how and why do material production and the social relations of production change? What distinguished Marx and Engels' answers to this question was their adoption of a materialist philosophy (see Chapter 1): the reality of the world around us is a material one that we perceive and study through our senses, rather than one in which ideas floated independently in the air. Thought cannot be separated from 'matter that thinks' (Rigby 1992: 104), and ideas cannot be understood outside of their material, social and cultural contexts (e.g. compare the prevailing ideas in the ancient world with those under capitalism). Humans do not respond mechanistically and passively to stimuli from the world around them, nor are their being, ideas and attitudes made by God. The starting point of any study of human societies is economic and social life (Box 2.1).

This argument does not mean that ideas are unimportant, rather they have to be seen in their historical and social contexts. The

---

BOX 2.1 MARX AND ENGELS' MATERIALIST PHILOSOPHY

The classic statement of Marx and Engels' materialism was written in 1845:

> We do not set out from what men say, imagine, conceive, nor from men as narrated, thought of, imagined, conceived, in order to arrive at men in the flesh. We set out from real, active men ... (who) ... developing their material production and their material intercourse, alter, along with their real existence, their thinking and the products of their thinking. Life is not determined by consciousness, but consciousness by life.

They continue by stating

> the first premise of all human existence and, therefore, of all history, is namely, that men must be in a position to live in order to be able to "make history". But life involves before everything else eating and drinking, a habitation, clothing and many other things. The first historical act is thus the production of the means to satisfy these needs, the production of material life itself.

(1970: 47–8)

material factors of production do not determine the social relations by which this production is controlled and distributed: they set limits on each other and change comes about through contradictions between them. Similarly, the economic **base** (which includes material and social production) does not determine forms of social institutions, politics, legal structures, ideologies (see below), art forms, etc. (what was called by Marx the **superstructure**). There is 'considerable scope for political and ideological factors to develop according to their own rhythms, and to react back on to the economy' (Callinicos 1999: 112 ff.). There is also scope for a variety of contingent factors (e.g. environmental change) to contribute to the specific development of social change. Societies with the same material basis may have a variety of social relations, ideologies and so on.

Marx and Engels' materialist conception of history is both a philosophical argument and an intellectual map of how historical analysis should proceed. Society is viewed as a whole, a totality. Rather than its parts being harmoniously in balance, there is constant change, conflict and contradiction (e.g. between the forces and relations of production, the base and the superstructure, capitalists and the working class). The outcome of these contradictions and conflicts is transformation within, and of, society, rather than change being determined by external factors. Change occurs within specific historical contexts and does not have predictable directions. Marx never presented this **dialectic** in detail and opinions differ as to whether it is a method of study or a theory, and how far it can be applied to the natural, as well as the human, world (see McGuire 2008: 74 for a basic introduction and 2002: 91–115 for a more detailed presentation).

HUMAN BEINGS MAKE HISTORY

Within this conception of history, there is an active role for human beings: they are not 'simply played like mere chessmen by the economic conditions' (Engels quoted in Rees 1994: 69).

> History is nothing but the succession of the separate generations, each of which exploits the materials, the capital funds, the productive

forces handed down to it by all preceding generations, and thus, on the one hand, continues the traditional activity in completely changed circumstance and, on the other, modifies the old circumstances with a completely changed activity.

(Marx and Engels 1970: 57)

Human beings continually and actively contribute to the making of history. As Marx (2010: 15) puts it, 'men make their own history, but they do not make it just as they please; they do not make it under circumstances chosen by themselves, but under circumstances directly encountered, given and transmitted from the past'. They are not freewheeling individuals, but born into social structures that enable and constrain them from acting in particular ways (Callinicos 1987).

OUR CONSCIOUSNESS OF REALITY

The focus of almost all Marx and Engels' work was on capitalism and the class structure by which capitalist societies were organised, hence their resounding opening sentence in *The Communist Manifesto* (Marx and Engels 1998: 34): 'the history of all hitherto existing society is the history of class struggle'. The contradictions between the forces and relations of production were acted out between classes, whose consciousness of the 'struggle' was conditioned by their position within it. The security of the dominant class in any society was not just about controlling the means of production and exercising physical coercion over the exploited classes.

The class which has the means of material production at its disposal, has control at the same time over the means of mental production, so that thereby, generally speaking, the ideas of those who lack the means of mental production are subject to it.

(Marx and Engels 1970: 64)

The interests of the dominant class are represented as those of the whole society. There is a false relationship between the reality of daily life and the consciousness or imagination of that life by exploited classes (**ideology**).

WORK FOR HUMANITY

The theoretical arguments and concepts introduced by Marx and Engels were not presented in philosophical isolation. As Marx (see Marx and Engels 1970: 123) put it in the famous eleventh of his *Theses on Feuerbach*, 'the philosophers have only *interpreted* the world, in various ways; the point is to *change* it'. Elsewhere he urged scientists to 'work for humanity' (see Fromm 1969: 222). His work was done for a purpose, not only to understand the workings of capitalist society, but to put that understanding to use in changing that society. Marx and Engels' materialist philosophy was 'the scientific theory of working-class emancipation' (Callinicos 1983: 8), revealing, for example, the nature of ideological coercion, and participating in political movements and action. They were by no means politically neutral. Rather than think in terms of separate domains of 'theory' and 'practice', Marx argued that they were united in what was called **praxis**, or practice that was theoretically informed. Praxis was a dialectical process between knowing the world, subjecting that knowledge to vigorous criticism, and then using that knowledge in action to change the world. Knowledge was no good for its own sake (for a clear presentation of Marx's praxis, see Patterson 2009: 57–62).

STUDYING NONCAPITALIST SOCIETIES

If the social, economic and political structures, coupled with the values, of capitalism were not an inevitable outcome of humanity but a product of history, then it became important to study earlier forms of human society. But while there were historical sources, of variable quantity and quality, on feudal and classical societies in Europe, the study of 'primitive' societies was only just beginning in mid- to late nineteenth-century anthropology. Marx admired Darwin's evolutionary theory, and he was also aware of the study of prehistory, and studied different forms of tribal societies in his 1857–8 notebooks: his proposals for historical periods dominated by specific modes of production were not intended as rigid, unilineal sequences, but as 'a very rough and provisional hypothesis of historical development' (Hobsbawn in Marx 1964: 32).

Stimulated by the American anthropologist Lewis Henry Morgan's research on stages (based on productive technology) in social development, Marx compiled his *Ethnological Notebooks* in

1880–2 (Krader 1972). This manuscript formed the source for Engels' (1972, originally published in 1884)) book on *The Family, Private Property and the State*. The outcome of these works was patchy in scale and content. Although criticised for the way that they used the concepts and methods of analysis for class structures under capitalism, the overall record of Marx and Engels was in proposing a materialist conception of history that was not predestined to proceed in any one direction (**non-teleological**). It placed ideas and human nature in their historical contexts, studied production and reproduction, proposed a non-determinist method for historical analysis, advocated a commitment to do science to change the world and provided the basis for a tradition of thought and action in the following century. As McGuire (2002: 9) puts it,

> Marxism is not a single, coherent theory of society that can be hitched to our purposes or dismissed in a few terse sentences. It is, instead, a philosophy, a tradition of thought, a mode of theoretical production, which has produced, and will produce, many theories.

THE MARXIST TRADITION

After the deaths of Marx and Engels, there were important debates on whether to change society by democratic reform or by revolution, as in the works of Lenin (1917) and Rosa Luxemburg (Scott 2008). Other strands of thought embraced biological and technological determinism, as well as the inevitability of evolutionary progress through the same successive, economic stages (**fatalism**) (McClellan 1998). By the end of the 1920s, Stalin was using Marxism as 'an ideological weapon used to justify, *a posteriori*, the politics of the Soviet regime', with rigid stages of social evolution, an unintelligible 'dialectical' method, and a rigid orthodoxy that repressed creative thought (Blackledge 2006: 77–8). The critical and nuanced thought of Marx was transformed into doctrine in the USSR and Eastern Europe until the 1950s.

CLASS CONSCIOUSNESS, CULTURE AND CRITICAL THEORY

The political reordering of Western and Central Europe following the Great War, along with failed revolutions (e.g. in Germany) and the repressive orthodoxy of Stalinism, shaped an intellectual reaction to deterministic and evolutionary approaches to historical change. In what became known much later in the 1950s as **Western Marxism** (Therborn 2010: 87), attention was diverted from economic relations to the cultural superstructure. Georg Lukács (1923) reaffirmed Marx's belief in the unity of theory and practice and the role of human action in social change, and developed Marx's ideas on **class consciousness**. While Russian Marxists focused on the economic 'base' of societies, the Italian Antonio Gramsci (Jones 2006) rejected any economic determinism, gave equal weight to culture, politics and ideology and is not for nothing called 'the theoretician of the superstructure' (McLellan 1998: 197). Like Lukacs, his Marxism was 'a practical activity rather than a disinterested pursuit of knowledge' (Beteille 2008: 60). A political prisoner for a decade from 1926, his ideas were developed in 34 notebooks (not published until 1971) and written without full access to sources and to avoid the scrutiny of censorship. Gramsci's central and most famous concept is that of **hegemony**, for which he offered more than one definition. Following Marx, he argued that physical coercion was insufficient for ruling classes to establish and maintain their dominance of lower classes. Ideology, expressed culturally and symbolically in the ideas, or worldviews, of the dominant classes, portrays their ideas and interests as those of the whole society. They are seen as natural and unquestionable, thereby supporting their coercion. However, Gramsci did not subscribe to this thesis, arguing that lower classes were not cultural dupes and were able (through the actions of what he called 'organic intellectuals') to develop their own world views. Hegemony was fragile and more dynamic than allowed for in what is called a dominant ideology thesis.

The cultural superstructure was also a focus of the Frankfurt School, based in Frankfurt's Institute for Social Research (founded in 1923) and reassembled in Los Angeles after its Jewish members fled the Nazi regime before World War II. The work of individuals such as Max Horkheimer, Theodor Adorno and Herbert Marcuse focused on themes such as the extent to which claims to knowledge about society are shaped by their social and class contexts and whose interests these claims serve (**critical theory**), the role of human action in determining history, how mass culture (e.g. in music and art) helps to legitimate domination (both in Fascist Germany and consumerist North America), and how Marxism could be integrated with other philosophies or academic schools of thought such as psychoanalysis (see McClellan 1998: 283–307; Callinicos 2007: 246–57). In contrast to 'classical' Marxism, the absence of political activism separated these academics from the working class and theory from practice, while class structure and political economy were largely neglected.

REVISITING MARX, PLURALISM AND PRECAPITALIST SOCIETIES

Since the end of World War II, Marxism has passed through cycles of popularity and marginalisation: as Paul Foot (2012: 432) puts it 'Each generation of intellectuals buries (Marx), and then exhumes him in order to bury him again', especially given wider political contexts such as the end of Stalinism, the fragmentation of the USSR, and the dominance of neoliberal economics in the Western world since the 1980s. One should not also underestimate the importance of the wider availability of translations (some for the first time) of the early works of Marx and Engels: the ability to engage more informatively, and in a more nuanced way, with the arguments contained in these 'classic texts' and the works of authors such as Luxemburg and Gramsci, contributed to the discard of the repressive Stalinist orthodoxy. Within the social sciences (including anthropology and archaeology) the major period of Marx's 'exhumation' was in the late 1960s–the early 1980s, while he was a 'dead dog' (Callinicos 2007: 261) from the mid-1980s to early 1990s. But in all periods, there were mainly academic theorists who were called 'Marxists' of some kind, or who looked for dialogues with a stunning range of social and philosophical approaches, while others rejected some or all of Marx's central ideas. Pluralism characterised positions taken by those within the Marxist tradition (see Spriggs 1984: 2 on different views of Marx's materialism) and interaction between them and other theories (e.g. structuralism – see Chapter 4).

A good example of debate and discard centred on the work of the French philosopher Louis Althusser, who played a pivotal role in a revision of Marx and Engels' ideas on historical change, placing the emphasis on the relations of production as determinants of social change. This presentation of history as 'a process without a subject' (Althusser 1972: 183) removed the roles of human beings and contingency in social change. Existing social relations were reproduced through ideologies, but as critics pointed out, it is one thing to reproduce existing social relations, but another to change them into new forms of such relations. Also, Althusser's argument does not show how ideologies are imposed on people (Callinicos 1976: 62). Although he recognised the existence of class struggle, this conflicted with his conception of history as 'a process without a subject'. This debate about the relative roles of social structures and individual action in historical change continued (see Chapter 4) in the works of both Marxist and non-Marxist writers from the 1970s.

Debates on key Marxist concepts and analysis of precapitalist societies permeated the work of French anthropologists (e.g. Maurice Godelier), and those influenced by them, for two decades from the mid-1960s (Bloch 1985: 141–72), as part of an attempt to reform classical Marxism. What are modes of production and how useful are they for studying such societies? How do social relations of production shape the forces of production, rather than the other way round? What is class and can the concept be applied to all societies, not just to those under capitalism? How far did the economic base of societies determine the superstructure? How far could precapitalist societies be studied as isolated from webs and networks of such societies across regions and continents? Two approaches (see Gosden 1999: 109) were to become particularly influential in both anthropology and (later) archaeology: the first linked social power in non-class societies to control of high-ranking exchange rather than basic production; the second situated local sequences of social change within larger-scale, regional and inter-regional 'world systems' through the movement of goods and people. A distinctive strand of Marxist feminism, focusing on gender inequality and stimulated ultimately by Engels' (1972) book *The Origin of the Family, Private Property, and the State*, also developed within (and beyond) anthropology (e.g. Leacock 1983). These debates and developments took place within the context of what had been a massive change in knowledge of precapitalist societies during the twentieth century.

While government based on socialist politics is now more of a rarity across the world, Marxist theory and ideas remain highly influential (although not always explicitly so) in the social and historical sciences. Therborn (2010: 157–78) traces a range of 'current left theoretico-political positions' including Marxist and non-Marxist thought, the former including a 'resilient Marxism' that beats the drum of the 'classic' sources (e.g. Alex Callinicos, Perry Anderson), and a post-Marxism of 'writers with an explicitly Marxist background, whose recent work has gone beyond Marxist problematics and who do not publicly claim a continuing Marxist commitment' (Therborn 2010: 165). Marxism has not ceased to exist. The term 'Marxian' is also in evidence to refer to the use of Marxist ideas in the absence of political commitment to radical, social and political change.

MARX, WEBER AND DURKHEIM

In contrast to Marx and the Marxist tradition, Durkheim's focus was on a functional rather than evolutionary analysis of human society, that is, thinking of society as an organism, with each part playing a (more or less) important and well-defined role in its survival. He conceived of society and its structures as being founded on, and unified by, religious values, beliefs and practices, with lesser importance being ascribed to the economic factors and class structures studied by Marx. Unlike Marx, Durkheim respected the institution of the state and conceived of society and its structures as being 'the unintended consequences of human actions' (Callinicos 2007: 131), rather than a more nuanced outcome of interaction between individuals, social groups and pre-existing social structures (see below). Weber also favoured such **methodological individualism** (Box 4.2) and the functional role of religious beliefs, values and practices in social integration. He contrasted stratified social and economic classes with what he called differences of status, which have claims of social esteem based on such factors of lifestyle, education, occupation or inheritance. If there was one factor, above all others, which for Weber was central to all social life it was power, based in different circumstances on economic relations, social status or what he called 'prestige' (for Weber, a positively valued status).

The influence of the thinking of Marx, Durkheim and Weber can be seen in the subsequent history of social theory through to the present day, whether their work has been built upon or discarded (at least for periods of time) (Callinicos 2007). Durkheim's functional analysis of societies as organised like the human body was influential on both British social anthropologists such as Malinowski and

Radcliffe-Brown and the American sociologist Talcott Parsons from the 1910s to the 1950s. Examples of Weber's legacy can be seen in the works of anthropologists and sociologists such as Michael Mann and Anthony Giddens (Callinicos 2007: 263–64), both of whom continue the stance against Marxism that was seen in Weber's original work, favouring an account of social change emerging from the interaction between different forms of power (political, economic and ideological), as is best seen in Mann's books on social power (e.g. 1986).

MARXISM IN ARCHAEOLOGY

IN AND OUT OF THE CLOSET?

What impact has Marxism had on archaeology? As Patterson (2003: 1) puts it, archaeologists have had 'conversations' with Marx's ghost that have been characterised 'by genuine dialogue, by backtalk and crosstalk and by silence, disregard, avoidance and suppression' (to which we might add appropriation and misrepresentation). Marxism in archaeology has been in and out of the theoretical closet, rejected as a dangerous imposition of politics on archaeological interpretation, yet plundered for useful ideas that are blended with ideas from other intellectual traditions. Marxism is everywhere and nowhere, framed in what Trigger (1993: 174) called 'the disembedded and free-floating nature of Marxist ideas in western society'.

Informative histories of Marxism in regional archaeologies have been presented by McGuire (2002: 53–89; 2008) and Patterson (2003). Rather than repeat these histories I will focus on some key examples of Marxist archaeologies and the borrowing of Marxist ideas by 'other' archaeologies. As a gross generalisation, explicitly Marxist archaeologies (as opposed to 'under the radar' use of Marxist ideas) were rare outside Eastern Europe before the 1970s. The most notable exception was the Australian Gordon Childe (Box 2.2). While Childe's materialism may have anticipated processual archaeology in its focus on production and social organisation, there were many points of difference (e.g. processualism's claims for universal laws of human behaviour, and its rejection of archaeology as a historical discipline).

BOX 2.2 GORDON CHILDE'S MARXIST ARCHAEOLOGY

Childe was one of the most famous archaeologists of the twentieth century (see McNairn 1980; Trigger 1980a; Green 1981). His Marxism was visible in his publications from the 1930s to his death in 1957. He was stimulated by the development of a Marxist archaeology in Russia that used larger-scale excavation of settlements and cemeteries, coupled with analyses of artefact uses and distributions within such sites, to infer productive activities, social relations and stages of social evolution (see Trigger 2006: 326–44). But this stimulus did not amount to uncritical emulation.

Childe's theoretical basis lay in the available works of Marx and Engels, which were rarely quoted or cited in his publications. His Marxism was materialist, but not determinist (e.g. regarding the relations between forces and relations of production). He directed attention at ideological factors that could constrain change, rather than such change being inevitable: as he put it, 'history does not disclose an unfaltering march to a predetermined goal' (Childe 1947: 73). Human beings made history and were products of history. They perceived the world around them through cognition and acted on it through culture. Their actions also had unintended consequences. Historians (including archaeologists) were not unbiased, they were influenced by 'interests and prejudices' of their society, such as their class, their ethnicity or their religious beliefs (Childe 1947: 22). Archaeology was not pursued just for the sake of archaeologists, but for society as a whole: archaeological knowledge 'will not increase the production of bombs or butter', but 'may be useful in helping (us) to think more clearly and then behave more humanely' (Childe 1956: 127). His most famous use of Marxism was in the book *Scotland Before the Scots* (Childe 1946) which received the kind of critical reception that underlined the extent of his intellectual isolation among the hierarchy of UK archaeology.

In the 1970s and 1980s, Anglo-American archaeologists began to draw explicitly on a wider range of social theories, influenced by French anthropologists such as Claude Levi-Strauss, Godelier and Althusser, the American anthropologist Jonathan Friedman (e.g. 1974) and the American sociologist Immanuel Wallerstein's (1974) World Systems theory (see below) (for further references see Spriggs 1984: 6–7). Such archaeologists acknowledged Childe's legacy, drew upon Marxist and Structural Marxist approaches (e.g. Friedman and Rowlands 1978), theorised ideology (e.g. Miller and Tilley 1984; Leone *et al.* 1987) and the role of human agency in social change, and recognised the political nature of archaeological practice. While there was clearly an overlap with issues debated in postprocessualism, the works of Marx and Engels were not always cited. Marx's ghost was everywhere but the borrowing from the Marxist tradition of thought could be selective (e.g. both Hodder and Hutson 2003 and Johnson 2020 mainly focus on ideology). It has also been argued that 'many contemporary archaeologists, positivists, postmodernists, and feminists alike simply do not know that many of their key concepts and perspectives derive from Marxism' (McGuire *et al.* 2005: 356).

Committed Marxist archaeologists recognised differences of opinion over key concepts. For example, is the dialectic a method of study or a theory, and how far it can be applied to the natural, as well as the human, world (McGuire 2002: 91–115)? Archaeological case studies multiplied and refuted the claim that Marxist approaches are 'short on the handling of concrete archaeological data collected through fieldwork' (Renfrew and Bahn 2012: 473). Let us now look at five themes pursued in Marxist archaeologies.

PRODUCTION AND SOCIAL RELATIONS

Marxist archaeologists have studied the social production, distribution and consumption of food and objects made of a range of raw materials (e.g. Muller's 1997 major study of the Mississippian political economy in south-eastern North America c. 1050–1600 BC; Tosi's 1984 analysis of craft specialisation in third millennium BC state societies of the Turanian Basin to the north of the Arabian Gulf), as well as the reproduction of populations (the future labour force), their society and their culture. Whatever is produced requires socially organised labour (e.g. numbers of people, time and labour available given competing forms of production), raw materials and instruments of labour (through which energy transforms raw materials). Whatever is produced has a social value, acquired from the social labour used in its production and from the use of products in satisfying specific needs. A key question that is asked by Marxist archaeologists is this: do all members of society play an equal part in production and in their access to the outcomes of that production? For example, are there social groups who consume more than they have invested, physically and mentally, in productive activities? Are the products of the labour appropriated by the few from the many? This would amount to 'surplus' production (which in non-Marxist thought usually refers to overall production greater than needs) and exploitation. The best introduction to these concepts is given by Risch (2008), while Delgado Raack and Risch (2008) present a case study illustrating how they can be used to analyse the social organisation of metal production (Box 2.3)

BOX 2.3 PREHISTORIC METAL PRODUCTION AND SOCIAL RELATIONS IN SOUTHEAST SPAIN

What were the uses and social values of early metal objects, and what can their study tell us about the societies that produced, used and discarded them? These questions have been asked of centres of early metallurgy in both the Old and New Worlds. One such centre is southeast Spain, where isolated copper production has been claimed for the mid-fifth millennium BC and more widespread, well-founded evidence for such production from the third millennium BC. From c. 2200 BC to 1550 BC, in the Argaric group of the Early Bronze Age, there were greater concentrations of weapons, tools and ornaments of copper and ornaments of silver and even gold. Their discovery in intra-mural, mainly individual, tombs has played a central role in debates on the nature of Argaric society.

Delgado Raack and Risch (2008) acknowledge the value of typo-logical and provenance analyses of these metal objects, but ask what we can learn about their production (e.g. successive stages, tools used, location) and the social relations of that production (e.g. was the distribution and consumption of metal objects prac-tised equally by all members of society?). Their focus is on the macro-lithic stone tools used as instruments of production. These tools are divided into three main classes: casting tools (moulds), forging tools (hammers, anvils) and polishing, cutting and sharpening tools (including slabs and plaques). Tools of each class are analysed for their overall morphology, their geology (distance found from sources, appropriateness for production tasks), morphology of the active surface, production traces (use-wear analysis) and 'validating information' (e.g. experimental replications, contextual data).

For the Copper Age site of Cerro de la Virgen, such evidence for metal production was concentrated in one open-air area enclosed by structures that were not distinguished by features that might suggest unequal access to metallurgy. 'The distribution of sharpening plaques inside and outside many buildings further suggests that the produced metal tools were used and maintained by all members of the community' (2008: 245). Along with the distribution of metal objects 'and other materials of a high social value' this suggests the absence of social relations of class. In contrast, the data analysed from the later, Argaric site of Fuente Alamo do support the interpretation of 'an emerging dominant class' (2008: 247) on a regional level, with all the stages of metal production no longer being carried out equally on individual settlements.

PROPERTY, CLASS AND THE STATE

In contemporary Western society we commonly use the term 'property' to refer to individual ownership of commodities: for example, 'that is *my* mobile phone/tablet/pair of jeans'. At the same time, there are legal ways in which property *rights* are established and enforced, and property (e.g. houses, land) is passed between generations. Marxists talk about rights and relations not things, tracing the emergence of unequal social relations of control over the production, allocation, exchange and use of products. A famous distinction is often made between 'communal' and 'private' property relations. The material and social nature of production means that archaeologists have rich data with which to study property relations (e.g. Hunt and Gilman 1998; Lull *et al.* 2005).

The existence of surplus production, social exploitation and property relations implies the existence of societies structured by relations of class: as the ancient historian Ste-Croix put it 'class (essentially a relationship) is the collective social expression of the fact of exploitation, the way in which exploitation is embodied in a social structure' (1981: 43). Class societies are contrasted structurally with those based on relationships of kinship. The political and economic interests (e.g. property rights) of a dominant class (as, for example, in the ancient, feudal and capitalist worlds) are argued to be guaranteed by the institutions of the state and based on physical and ideological coercion. 'States are like the lids on pressure cookers. They attempt to control volatile, often explosive mixtures by keeping class antagonism and contradictions in check: they often fail' (Patterson 2003: 23). Archaeologists have emphasised the existence of the earliest state societies in the form of 'civilisations' such as those of Mesopotamia, Egypt, Mesoamerica, Peru, the Indus Valley and China, but placed greater weight on such defining characteristics as economic and political centralisation, bureaucracy and large-scale population densities, rather than the existence of class relations. These different views of class and state societies have provoked general and area-specific debates on when and where states or state-like societies appeared in the past (e.g. Saitta 1992; Chapman 2008; Lull and Micó 2011). Routledge (2014) also provides an illustrated guide to state theory and the use of Gramsci's concept of hegemony in our understanding of states.

LARGE-SCALE ECONOMIC AND POLITICAL SYSTEMS

If societies divided by relations of class were a relatively late development in human history, how were pre-class societies organised? Can Marxist theories developed for the study of capitalism be applied to earlier societies? At what scale(s) (e.g. local, regional) should they be studied? These kinds of questions were posed initially by a group of French anthropologists in the 1960s and applied in archaeology from the second half of the 1970s. Major changes in production, especially of subsistence, were now attributed to social practices such as rituals, feasting and exchange (e.g. Bender 1978 on the adoption of agriculture): the social relations shaped the forces of production rather than the other way round. Major social, economic and political changes also took place in larger-scale networks, rather than the smaller-scale, independent changes studied by processual archaeology.

In societies organised by kinship relations of production and reproduction, the flows of goods, especially 'prestige' goods (rare craft products that were highly ranked), in competitive exchange, were used to obtain more wives in marriage and thereby increase the demographic reproduction of social groups. Susan Frankenstein and Michael Rowlands (1978) proposed such a **prestige goods** model to explain the development and decline of Iron Age societies in south-western Germany in the context of wider social, economic and political changes in neighbouring areas of central and Mediterranean Europe. Local chiefs were able to use such access to local and (increasingly) regional prestige goods to invest in marital alliances and build up their 'demographic strength', competing with each other to establish social and political hierarchies in south-western Germany during the Early Iron Age. Ultimately the loss of control over the exchange of prestige goods led to the collapse of these hierarchies and their long-distance networks. This model was highly influential for a decade, but there have also been criticisms of its assumptions and applications (e.g. Gosden 1985; Moffett and Chirikure 2016 on the Southern African Iron Age). Positive examples of the study of prestige goods in Pacific archaeology have also been published recently (Earle and Spriggs 2015).

The regional and inter-regional scales of the prestige goods model also drew on the sociologist Wallerstein's (1974) analysis of the rise of capitalism as a world economy from the sixteenth century AD. This focused on the movement (e.g. through trading posts and colonies) of staple goods and raw materials from peripheral regions such as the Indian subcontinent to their dominant consumers in core regions such as Western Europe. The relationship between the 'core' region of the Mediterranean and the 'periphery' of south-central Europe in the Early Iron Age was essential to Frankenstein and Rowlands's prestige goods model. The strengths and weaknesses of Wallerstein's **world systems** model for noncapitalist societies have been debated in case studies since the 1980s (e.g. Rowlands *et al.* 1987; Parkinson and Galaty 2009) (Box 2.4). The weight of criticism led to the reframing of 'world systems theory' as 'world systems analysis', an intellectual tool for large-scale analysis of how societies interact with each other and what the outcomes of that interaction might be. As McGuire (2002:79) points out, a North American 'world systems' approach has been 'stripped of its Marxist foundation': he reclaims this foundation by using the concepts of production, distribution, exchange and consumption to analyse social reproduction within the context of larger scale systems of social, economic and political relationships (1989: 40).

BOX 2.4 TWO EXAMPLES OF WORLD SYSTEMS IN EUROPE

Archaeological applications of world systems theory to later prehistoric Europe present us with the relationship between a European 'periphery' beyond a Near Eastern urban 'core'. Sherratt and Sherratt's (1993) study of the Mediterranean economy is a schematic mapping of four stages of the development of core and periphery from c. 3500 BC to 500 BC, with the 'urbanised manufacturing zone with bulk transport and state organisation' reaching the Aegean by 1500 BC and southern and eastern Spain by c. 500 BC.

Kristiansen (1998) argues in detail for a world-system of the Near East, the Mediterranean and Europe from c. 2200 BC. Social reproduction operated at a larger, and more uncontrollable, scale than that of people's everyday lives. For example,

> the expansion of international exchange accelerated the pace of change in regional cultural traditions and – by the very nature of bronze technology – created a dependency in terms of supplies of metal and know-how between different regions that added a new dimension to change and tradition.
>
> (1998: 3)

The Mycenaeans had a central role as 'transmitters and receivers of new influences between the east Mediterranean and central Europe' (1998: 361) and the establishment of trade contacts with the west Mediterranean (although the archaeological data makes the latter linkage difficult to sustain – see Blake 2008).

IDEOLOGY

The exercise of power to establish, maintain and change political, economic and social systems, at whatever scale, is much mentioned and debated within archaeology and, more generally, in the social sciences. In works in the Marxist tradition, these debates have centred on the use of physical and ideological coercion. Ideology is thought of as 'an active component of social relations, and as a product of fundamentally unequal power relations that serves to maintain, advance, legitimate, and obscure inequality and exploitation' (Bernbeck and McGuire 2011a: 46). Whether we are in school, or a place of worship, a festival of remembrance, or other state rituals, we are exposed from childhood to the dominant ideas of our society. Some ideologies of modern nation states stress equality (think of France) or equality of opportunity (the American dream), but exhibit highly unequal social relations, while an emphasis on democracy may obscure undemocratic practices. In all cases, these ideologies express the interests of a particular group or groups as common to all or many groups in society and 'maintain, advance, legitimate, and obscure inequality and exploitation'. They are central to relations of power and domination. Ideologies are not necessarily either 'true' or 'false', nor are they blindly accepted by the exploited and dominated, who may reshape them as a form of resistance. The degree of correspondence between ideologies and people's everyday lives, actions and social experience contributes to their degrees of acceptance and resistance.

Marxist archaeologists ask two important questions: how far do modern ideologies contribute to our framing of research topics and questions and the ways in which the past is represented to the public (e.g. via television programmes, museum displays, heritage and tourist sites); and how do we study the role of ideologies in the histories of societies (Box 2.5)?

The productivity of Marxist studies of ideology in archaeology has been criticised by Hodder and Hutson (2003: 79–89), who argue that these studies ignore the specific forms taken by ideologies and how particular ideologies came into being. They also question the extent to which we can make a clear distinction between ideology and social 'reality': 'since reality has to be perceived and created by the observer, it is itself ideology' (2003: 84).

BOX 2.5 ARCHAEOLOGY AND IDEOLOGY

Mark Leone *et al.* (1987) focus attention on the relationship between our knowledge of the past and the contexts of its production, how archaeologists might challenge people's understandings of their history and how it has been produced. Annapolis is a city in Maryland, founded in the mid-seventeenth century AD and with a history that was locally written from the 1880s to attract both businesses and tourists. This history was exclusive rather than inclusive, and compiled almost exclusively by white historians. It is not surprising that black history was less evident, separate from white history, and omitted a record of slavery and how it shaped the development of social, economic and political relations between black and white inhabitants in Annapolis. The history was partial and selective. The research by Leone and his co-researchers used archaeological excavations and historical records to challenge this history. They also organised site tours to challenge locals' and visitors' knowledge of local history, to show how the city's ideology masked the reality of its past, and to help visitors to develop a critical understanding of how archaeologists work, interpret and present the past.

Paynter and McGuire (1991) focus on ideologies of domination and resistance, and their cultural expression in a range of material contexts, from pottery and food consumption to cemeteries and the construction, use and destruction of monuments such as pyramids and megalithic tombs. McGuire's analysis of late seventeenth- to twentieth-century AD cemeteries in Broome County, upstate New York produced interesting observations on the changing relationship between the dominant ideology and inequalities:

> In each time period, the cemeteries provided a material form that affirmed and legitimated the dominant ideology of the period. In the early 19th century, the cemetery denied the existence of inequalities in the community; in the late 19th and 20th century it naturalized existing inequalities in a glorification of individual success; and in the mid to late 20th century, it denied the existence of qualitative differences between individuals.
>
> (1988: 457)

> For the same county's cemeteries, Wurst (1991) documented the
> nineteenth-century co-existence of rural and urban elite ideologies,
> the former 'actively minimized or ignored class differences' while the
> latter accentuated such differences. Further case studies on the ways
> in which archaeologists study past ideologies and how current ide-
> ologies shape the ways in which we produce knowledge of the past
> can be found in Bernbeck and McGuire (2011b: 40–58).

KNOWLEDGE, CRITICISM AND ACTION

As we saw earlier in this chapter, Marxists believe that knowledge
has to be put to use to criticise and take action in the world
(McGuire *et al.* 2005). Archaeologists may not be able to produce
the knowledge that will 'increase the production of bombs and butter', as Childe (1956: 127) wrote, or overthrow capitalism, but it
can be 'a powerful weapon in ideological struggles that have real
consequences for people' (McGuire 2008: 21). One such struggle is
over national identity: is the nation constant, 'a people…who share a
common language and culture, heritage and territory', or is national
identity 'created, contested and unstable', shaped by historical events
and processes but experienced differently by different social, ethnic
and other groups (McGuire 2008: 23)? The second of these answers
can help destabilise extreme nationalist movements based on mythical pasts and unsound use of historical and archaeological evidence
(see McGuire 2008: 23–8 for examples).

There are enough examples of archaeology and history being
rewritten and used to support political agendas (e.g. Nazi Germany)
to raise challenging questions about the interests served by knowledge of the past. Trigger (1980b, 1984) argued that stereotypes of
indigenous North American peoples as inherently 'simple' and
'uncivilised' underlay archaeological interpretations of their lack
of social and cultural development, thus justifying the annexation
of their lands (what Trigger called, 'colonialist' archaeology). He
also argued that archaeology has historically been a middle-class
profession reflecting middle-class interests (e.g. the emergence of
archaeology in the nineteenth century showing how technological progress, on which the industrial revolution was based, 'was the

continuation of what had been going on more slowly throughout human history', Trigger 1984: 364). This requires us to reflect critically on our theories and interpretations, as well as our choices of research topics, as we engage with the material world of archaeological remains and its constraints.

If archaeology produces understandings of the past, then it should also aim to be 'emancipatory' (Saitta 2007: 3). Instead of top-down histories that privilege elites, rulers and the wealthy, we should challenge assumptions on class, gender and ethnic identities and relations (e.g. they are not constant or determined by human nature), make such relations more visible in our interpretations and give groups such as the working classes and indigenous peoples greater participation in the choice and pursuit of archaeological research. Archaeological and ethnohistoric research can make important contributions to claims over land and resources by indigenous people. Working classes are less visible in archaeological practice and often cut off from access to archaeological knowledge and debate by the style in which it is written. As the work of the Ludlow Collective has shown (Box 2.6), archaeology can make important contributions to working-class history and consciousness.

BOX 2.6 LUDLOW AND WORKING-CLASS HISTORY

The Colorado coalfield strike (for full details of the history and archaeology, see Saitta 2007) took place in 1913–14 and was an important event in American labour history. Local resistance to exploitative employment and working conditions culminated in a refusal by employers to recognise the United Mine Workers of America. Miners were ejected from their company homes and set up tented camps. The mine owners brought in replacement miners, harassed the strikers and violence broke out. The state militia was brought in by the state governor, attacked a miner's tent colony at Ludlow (killing 25 men, women and children in one day) and was resisted by the miners in pitched battles over a ten-day period. The strike continued until the end of 1914, when the union ended the struggle.

Starting out from documentary records, a programme of five seasons of archaeological survey and excavations (mainly at Ludlow) focussed on questions of community location and layout, ethnic organisation, the use of cellars dug beneath tents, and study of the diet and material culture of the miners. This fieldwork aimed to answer questions on topics such as class solidarity, how the miners supported themselves during the strike, and how class consciousness was fostered in a context of ethnic diversity; in general what were the 'strategies that workers used to resist exploitation, build solidarity across ethnic boundaries, make a living while out on strike, and interrelate with wider communities' (Saitta 2007: 64)? Not only did the archaeologists aim to contribute to knowledge of the history of unionism and industrial struggle locally in southeast Colorado, but also to involve the modern, working-class communities of the Ludlow region in developing and honouring the history of unionism and the struggle for workers' rights in this region. The archaeologists worked with descendants of those killed in the Ludlow massacre, welcomed the local community to the excavations as visitors and participants, gave talks to community and workers' groups, exhibited finds, engaged with local media and took part in the annual Ludlow memorial service.

This 'collective action' brought together archaeologists and the working class in an affirmation of public memory and working-class identity, as well as a contradiction of the North American ideology of a classless society. The knowledge produced by archaeology contributes to the weakening of that ideology and the emancipation of the working class.

MARX'S LEGACY: INESCAPABLE AND EVER-PRESENT

The legacy of Marx is alive and kicking in archaeology. It is widely dispersed in different countries and different archaeologies; it is critical and self-critical, pluralistic and active, rather than a dogma that simply reiterates old texts. It is impossible to imagine the development of archaeological theory in the last five decades without Marxist ideas and concepts, whether they are explicit or hidden, developed in context or borrowed piecemeal. We need to recognise and counter the misunderstandings and misrepresentations of Marxist thought. We also have to engage with those who think that Marx is a very distant intellectual ancestor, whose thinking contains some dead wood that has to be removed from the Marxist tradition as a result of critique in the twentieth century.

If Marx's legacy to our study of past social structures and relations is inescapable and ever-present, what about the legacy of Charles Darwin, another intellectual titan of the nineteenth century, to the study of evolutionary thought in archaeology?

SUMMARY

- This chapter introduces the central ideas of Marxism and their history, before illustrating their impact on archaeological theory and practice.
- The key themes of Marx and Engels presented here are as follows: the nature of humans as natural, social and cultural beings; the importance and nature of production and reproduction in human societies; the materialist conception of history; the active role of humans as social beings in making history; the relationship between social reality and our consciousness of it and the importance of working to change the world rather than just understanding it.
- The Marxist tradition has produced examples of orthodox and dogmatic thinking, as well as less deterministic work on themes such as culture and class consciousness in varying cycles of popularity and isolation, as well as examples of pluralism that tried to integrate its ideas with those of other theoretical traditions.
- Marxism in archaeology has been both explicit and hidden, adopted as a whole or plundered for specific ideas.
- Explicit examples of Marxist approaches in Western archaeology were comparatively rare during the period of processual archaeology in the 1960s–1970s.
- From the mid-1970s, Marxist archaeologists have studied topics such as production and social relations; property, class and the state; prestige economies and world systems; ideology and reflexive approaches to the history and practice of archaeology.
- Postprocessual archaeology drew on ideas and concepts from the recent Marxist tradition, as well as from a wider range of social theories.
- Marxist perspectives within a political economy perspective continue to develop in the twenty-first century.

FURTHER READING GUIDE

Berlin (1978) and Hunt (2009) provide the best biographies of the lives and works of Marx and Engels, while basic introductions to those works, in their intellectual and political contexts, are published by Callinicos (1999) and Hands (2015). Derber's (2011) imaginary conversation with Marx's ghost is an accessible debate on the key ideas and their relevance to the modern world. McLellan (1998) and McGuire (2002: 21–51) offer readable guides to the international history of the Marxist tradition after Marx's death, while Therborn (2010) discusses Marxist thought at the beginning of the twenty-first century. Marxism and Marxist ideas in archaeology are generally not well covered in introductory texts, but a combination of McGuire (2002) and Patterson (2003, 2009) will give you the most comprehensive coverage. Bernbeck and McGuire (2011b) is the best recent work on ideology. Rosenswig and Cunningham (2017b) have edited detailed studies on modes of production in archaeology. The majority of the examples and case studies of Marxist archaeologies in this chapter are drawn from prehistory. For those of you interested in the classical world, Faulkner (2001) offers a radically different view of 'the grandeur that was Rome' in his study of exploitation and oppression in Roman Britain, while Matthews *et al.* (2002) present details and examples of Marxist approaches in North American historical archaeology.

3

EVOLUTIONARY THOUGHT
AND THE LEGACY OF DARWIN

Although Marxist theory has had its ups and downs in popularity, there is no doubting its significance and its long-term presence in the social sciences and archaeology as a theory of social relations. A similar history concerns ideas of the cultural and biological evolution of human beings, and the societies in which they lived, as the study of the human past unfolded over the last two centuries. In this chapter, we will examine evolutionary thought, its popularity and impact on archaeology during that period of time.

THE ORIGIN OF SPECIES

The usual starting point for any discussion of evolution is Charles Darwin's *Origins of Species* (1859). The argument on which his theory (what he called 'descent with modification') was based is simply expressed: there is variation between populations of individual organisms in all species, and this variation is inherited from generation to generation subject to the process of natural selection. This process includes a 'struggle for survival': individual variations, and ultimately species as a whole, may emerge or disappear as a result of the ability of organisms to adapt to their environments and the capacity of those environments to support them. Given the numbers of species, their fossil remains and the nature of natural selection, Darwin argued that biological evolution had to have been a slow, long-term, process. Although he proposed that individual variation was based on sexual reproduction, it took nearly another 100 years for scientists to show how hereditary information was carried genetically from one generation to another.

DOI: 10.4324/9781315657097-3

Darwin's theory of evolution was the product of almost three decades of research in the field (including his famous expedition on HMS Beagle from 1831 to 1836) and his study, and became his contribution to the wider debate between scientists and the Victorian Church about creation and the development of the natural world. Although he hardly mentioned our place in evolution until his book *The Descent of Man* (1871), he had accepted this as early as 1839 and both his supporters and critics understood clearly the implications of Darwin's theory for the evolution of human beings (Desmond and Moore 1991). Darwin's argument for the long-term span of animal, plant and, by implication, human evolution, provided independent support for Sir Charles Lyell's long geological time span for the history of the earth. The discoveries in 1859 of well-documented associations between extinct animal bones and human-made stone tools in the Windmill Cave at Brixham in Devon and the Abbeville gravels of northern France produced another line of evidence in support of greater human antiquity.

EVOLUTIONARY SEQUENCES OF CULTURE

A tradition of cultural evolution preceded and overlapped with Darwin's publication of his theory of biological evolution. Within eighteenth-century Enlightenment thought, scholars explored the relationship between nature and culture (e.g. between the environment and social customs and institutions), as well as the historical development of human societies (in contrast to earlier notions of a psychic unity of mankind). Explorations of, and contact with, non-Western societies were drawn upon in proposing evolutionary stages of past economies, social forms and institutions (e.g. Turgot's sequence of hunting, pastoral and agricultural societies; Miller's discussion of the evolution of the family, see Pluciennik 2005: 19–38). Such conjectural histories also permeated the nineteenth-century thought on legal systems, knowledge and belief systems, and broad, evolutionary sequences of human cultures exemplified in Lewis Henry Morgan's (1877) phases from Savagery to Barbarism to Civilisation (a strong influence on the later work of Marx and Engels). Evolutionary sequences (e.g. Stone-Bronze-Iron Ages) were also at the heart of archaeology's emergence as a field of study.

A key element of this early evolutionary thought was the linkage between evolution and complexity, most prominently seen in the work of Herbert Spencer, a key figure in the development of sociology. As Trigger (1998: 57) summarises Spencer's argument in the 1850s:

> the cosmos, plant and animal life, and human society had evolved in that order from simple, homogenous beginnings into increasingly differentiated, more complexly organised, and more intricately articulated entities ...Societies that were more complex and better integrated were able to prosper at the expense of less complex ones, just as human individuals and groups who were better adapted to social life supplanted those who were less well adapted.

Evolutionary arguments like these focused on directionality from simple to complex social structures and technologies.

Spencer's work also exemplified what became known later as **social Darwinism**: differences in individual human abilities to lead healthy, educated and profitable lives were regarded as a product of biological traits and not cultural opportunities during life. Biological differences were seen to determine cultural differences: whatever social changes took place, they were argued to have occurred naturally and very slowly. The application of evolutionary thought to human societies, especially the concept of the 'struggle for survival', was used to legitimise late nineteenth-century social, economic and political differences, including those that were ultimately racist and affirmed European dominance of the world (Trigger 1998: 63–82). For example, the so-called 'founding father' of field archaeology, General August Lane Fox Pitt Rivers, argued that changes in technology occurred in slow stages, showing the 'triumph' of objects of the greatest 'utility', in other words, the survival of the fittest (Bradley 1983). Pitt Rivers' conservative politics led him to use archaeology to uphold the hierarchical *status quo* of Victorian society and counter any thoughts among the populace of the desirability of revolutionary change. Not surprisingly, Marx praised Darwin for his unravelling of the laws of nature, but was sceptical of his evolutionary theory as a means to understand society and social change, shunning any notion of biological determinism.

NEO-EVOLUTIONISM

The late nineteenth and early twentieth centuries witnessed a marked decrease of anthropological and archaeological interest in generalised schemes of cultural evolution (e.g. Trigger 1998: 83–123). There was a shift to particularistic studies of spatial patterning in, and diffusion of, cultures. Cultural evolution received comparatively little attention until after World War II (with the notable exception of the Soviet straitjacket of pre-class, class and communist societies).

In North America, two anthropologists were key to the resurgence of cultural evolution within archaeology. Julian Steward had the most immediate impact, while Leslie White's impact was delayed until the emergence of processual archaeology. Steward (1955) worked with archaeologists on interactions between culture and environment from the north to the south of the American continent. He initially criticised archaeologists for their unambitious objectives, himself pursuing regularities in the development of cultures, wherever they were located, and how these regularities were related to the cultures' environments. If archaeologists were to understand social change, they needed to give particular attention to the cross-cultural ways in which culture (especially those 'core' features most closely related to subsistence and economy) adapted to environments through social behaviour, rather than study 'unique, historic and non-recurrent particulars' (quoted in Trigger 1998: 128). Science was opposed to history. Steward's approach (which he called **cultural ecology**) was a stimulus to archaeologists working on settlement patterns and ecology, especially in relation to the early civilisations of Mesoamerica and Peru, during the 1950s.

In contrast, White (1959) was interested in a more general evolution, that of culture rather than specific cultures, their environmental relations and their interactions. Culture was an adaptive system and evolved successfully (i.e. became more complex and more dominant) 'as the amount of energy harnessed *per capita* increases, or as the efficiency of putting energy to work is improved' (Trigger 1998: 127). In spite of its technological determinism, White's approach to culture was influential on Lewis Binford and early processual archaeology's study of cultural systems.

Abstract theory on culture was one thing, but how could anthropologists and archaeologists move to the specific and cross-cultural study of sequences of cultural evolution? The key publications were by two anthropologists, Elman Service and Morton Fried (for key aspects, see Table 3.1), who used cross-cultural studies to arrange societies from simple to complex (Chapman 2003: 34–8). Service (1962) focused on the structure of, and interpersonal relations within, society, using the ethnographic record to propose an evolutionary sequence

Table 3.1 Neo-evolutionary typologies

Elman Service (1962)	*Morton Fried (1967)*
Bands:	**Egalitarian societies**:
Hunter-gatherers	Hunter-gatherers/agriculturalists
Kinship relations and nuclear families	Division of labour by sex
Low population numbers and densities	Communal access to basic resources
	Situational leadership
	Low population densities
Tribes:	**Ranked societies**:
Agriculturalists	Agriculturalists
Increased sedentism	Ranking by ancestry in descent groups
Larger population sizes and densities	Equal access to basic resources
More non-residential groups	Division of labour by age/sex
Situational leadership	Inability to enforce authority
Self-sufficient residential groups	Equal participation in subsistence tasks
Situational leadership	
Egalitarianism	
Chiefdoms:	**Stratified societies**:
Further increase in population density	Status based on economic differences
Further increase in residential group size	Increased warfare
Increased productivity	
Centralised control + chiefs	
Specialisation + redistribution of produce	
Mobilisation of labour for public works	
Increased hierarchy + inequality	
States:	**States**:
Legitimised force	Class relations
Specialised bureaucratic government	
Further increases in complexity and inequality	

of societies, from hunting and gathering bands, to agricultural tribes, chiefdoms and states. Fried (1967) also produced a four-stage, evolutionary typology of societies, but this time giving greater weight to political factors. Instead of bands, Fried began with egalitarian societies, followed by ranked societies (instead of tribes and chiefdoms), stratified societies, and states. Both speculated on the reasons why they evolved from one type to another (see also Sahlins 1968 on the evolution of tribes to chiefdoms).

Within five years, Service (1967) had discarded the terms bands and tribes (in favour of 'egalitarian societies') and chiefdoms (replacing them with 'hierarchical societies', which now included the earliest states). Taken together these neo-evolutionary studies, when coupled with a more ambitious approach to the potential of archaeological data (e.g. mortuary and settlement analyses) stimulated processual archaeologists to make inferences on social types and their evolution in the past (e.g. Renfrew 1973 on chiefdoms in Neolithic and Early Bronze Age Wessex). The irony was such that neo-evolutionary research had a far greater impact on archaeology than on anthropology.

Social types were everywhere in the archaeology of the 1970s, but they were also criticised (for a summary, see Chapman 2003: 38–49). This was partly a question of how archaeologists could access the social in their data, and partly how the ethnographic record was used to define social types. Which societies did not fit into Service's typology? How many characteristics were needed to justify inclusion in a particular type? Were the typologies of Service and Fried sufficient to include all the variations in the ethnographic record? For example, chiefdoms were subdivided (e.g. simple/complex, group/individualising, collaborative/coercive) and nearly two dozen types of state society were defined (e.g. pristine/secondary/archaic/segmentary). What about the danger of imposing social types defined from the non-historical study of ethnography onto the archaeological record? The literature on cultural evolutionary thinking, its merits (e.g. as tools for thought) and demerits (e.g. non-historical, ethnocentric in their implication of directional change from the 'simple' past to the 'complex' present), multiplied (Chapman 2003: 50–9) in a context of theoretical interaction.

Thought about cultural evolution has diversified during the last four decades. Archaeologists no longer look simply to identify the presence/absence of social types in the past, but concepts such as 'chiefdoms' and 'states' remain in use as heuristic devices, starting points for historical and comparative research. Some archaeologists (e.g. Parkinson 2002) ask whether something is 'salvageable' in the concept of 'tribes', studying change at different scales in cultural processes or historical trajectories that may show cycles of greater or lesser equality through time. The retention of such ethnographically derived concepts is primarily known in North America, where new concepts such as 'transegalitarian societies' have been introduced in the study of inequalities and pathways to power (e.g. Hayden 1995). In contrast, such concepts are much less used in the UK, where reaction in postprocessual archaeology condemned the notion of cultural evolution as 'theoretically flawed and almost always (embodying) unwarranted ethnocentric evaluations' (Shanks and Tilley 1987b: 138).

Included within this dismissal was the concept of 'complexity'. Archaeologists educated within the neo-evolutionary approach still talk about 'complex societies' meaning chiefdoms and states, as opposed to hunter-gatherer bands and 'middle-range' societies such as tribes. But what is 'complexity'? Price (1995: 140) suggests that 'there seem to be as many definitions of complexity as there are archaeologists interested in the subject', but works with the definition 'things complex have more parts and more connections between parts'. In what ways are societies 'complex'? Are we talking about their social, political and economic structures, degrees of centralisation, hierarchies, ritual, belief systems, etc.? Archaeologists have moved away from looking to distinguish 'simple' and 'complex' societies, recognising that societies that used to be called 'simple' are complex in specific ways (e.g. their ritual practices, interpersonal and group networks).

NEO-DARWINISM AND DARWINIAN ARCHAEOLOGIES

Archaeologists were interested in relationships between culture and nature during the first half of the twentieth century, studying settlement distributions and environmental differences (e.g. soil types, cultivable land) and even arguing that the function of culture was to adapt to the constraints of the environment (e.g. Grahame

Clark's use of the ecosystem concept – Trigger 2006: 353–61). The theoretical context of these approaches changed dramatically after World War II to accommodate research on genetic inheritance and the evolutionary study of animal behaviour in what became known as **Neo-Darwinism**. These evolutionary studies of animal behaviour were extended to human beings; although we live in cultural worlds, we are also biological species.

But it was not until the late 1970s that an explicitly Darwinian approach was proposed for the study of the human past. Robert Dunnell (1978: 197) advocated an evolutionary archaeology

> as an explanatory framework that accounts for the structure and change evident in the archaeological record in terms of evolutionary processes (natural selection, flow, mutation, drift) either identical to or analogous with these processes as specified in neo-Darwinian evolutionary theory.

Dunnell's approach was very much out on a limb within archaeology, but it was the starting point for the development of what became known as Darwinian archaeologies, applying the central concepts of biological evolution to archaeological data (although not necessarily giving the same weight to all of these concepts). What are their basic principles and how are they used in archaeological research? Let us start with human ecosystems research (which was already established in processual archaeology when Dunnell's initial evolutionary work was published), and then continue with human behavioural ecology, cultural transmission and evolutionary psychology.

HUMAN ECOSYSTEMS

Modern ecological theory (Jones, M. 2005), like that adopted from botany by Clark in the 1930s, makes use of two key concepts, **ecosystem** and **adaptation**. The ecosystem includes human, animal and plant populations, as well as the habitats in which they live. These populations may share habitats or exist in specialised 'niches'. Whatever their subsistence strategies, human populations need to adapt to their habitats in order to survive. For example, their habitats may only be able to support specific sizes and densities of population given the available resources and the cultural means of exploiting them. Overall, the ecosystem is an analytical concept: there are social, economic and political networks that ensure that a culture within one ecosystem may be part of the environment of cultures in other ecosystems.

Adaptation has a key role in Darwinian evolution, but what kinds of questions are raised by its transfer to human populations? The social and cognitive abilities and structures that we possess have enabled us to develop the technologies to confront the challenges of inhospitable environments around the globe, as well as changes in those environments through time. Our capacity to produce the basic needs of existence exceeds that of all other animal species. We have developed the means to produce, harvest, store, transport and consume foods in an unrivalled way during the course of human and social evolution. But these 'successes' do not reduce culture to a simple mechanism of adaptation, nor can we say that it explains all changes in culture. Your clothing may functionally protect you and aid your survival in different climates, but the styles of such clothing say more about cultural and social factors than adaptation. Logos will not help you survive an arctic winter. Even if we argue that a given behaviour is adaptive, does this tell us how it came into existence and was widely adopted? Was the adoption of a particular behaviour adaptive for part or all the population? Roy Ellen (1982) discusses such questions and the uses of biological models in studying small-scale human societies, for example, calculating ecosystem carrying capacities and mapping the extraction, flow and consumption of energy from plant and animal resources in the ecosystem by local populations. Such ecosystems research has been one stimulus for the development of models of population sizes and densities, their changes through time and the causes and consequences of such changes. How far were these characteristics of populations controlled or regulated by cultural practices? What impacts did they have on changes in culture? How far did population growth and pressure play a causal part in technological or economic innovations (e.g. the adoption of agriculture)?

Archaeologists have used modern ecological theory to construct models of past cultures from hunter–gatherers to early states. Studies of Mesolithic ecosystems in Europe (Box 3.1) have been a stimulus to both thought and practice. A classic example of an ecosystems approach to the agricultural transition in Mesoamerica was presented by Kent Flannery (1968). Other big questions in archaeology concern the processes by which human colonisation took place, especially that of islands: was it coherent and purposeful, or piece-meal and accidental? by what phases did colonisation occur? what determined the long-term success of colonisation? what distinctive forms did island cultures take (e.g. the local types of monuments and cultural practices on islands as diverse as those of the Mediterranean and Polynesia) and how far were these shaped by their insularity? Answers to these questions have been sought through the theory of **island biogeography** (after MacArthur and Wilson 1967), which studies island ecosystems using the principles by which we anal-yse island plants and animals. Keegan and Diamond (1987) present an overview of evidence for island colonisation around the world, coupled with a comparative, biogeographical approach to the phases and processes of human colonisation. Kirch and Green (1987) focus on the factors that shape differences (e.g. degrees of isolation and external contact, specific colonisation processes) and similarities (e.g. demographic trends in, and cultural responses to, insular and confined locations) between island societies. The colonisation of Mediterranean islands and their subsequent cultural developments addresses similar issues (Box 3.2).

BOX 3.1 MESOLITHIC ECOSYSTEMS IN EUROPE

Two examples show the value of ecosystems models in the study of settlement and subsistence in Mesolithic Europe. David Clarke (1976) criticised the 'meat fixation' of archaeologists studying this area and period, and examined the sampling biases in the known site, artefact and faunal assemblages. He proposed that the largest proportion of the diet came from 'plant sources supple-mented by wider gathering and by hunting herbivorous mammals who themselves relied upon, and competed for, many of the same plant resources' (1976: 462). Clarke's ecological study of the *edible* productivity of European plant foods (1976: 463–7) showed latitudinal trends cross-cut by 'particularly productive geomor-phological and ecological sectors – the swamps, marshes, deltas, estuaries, lagoons, littoral zones, lakes, river and stream valleys, alluvial plains, and marine shallows'. Based on the premise that 'the distribution, territories and annual site systems of the Mesolithic communities of Europe must have been closely related to the edible productivity' (1976: 467) available to them, he used the ecological study to make some initial predictions on densities of populations and their organisation into seasonal territories (e.g. transhumant economies) in different locations of the continent. These predictions were then compared with the available archaeological evidence in Temperate and Mediterranean Europe. For the Mediterranean, Clarke also proposed that the adoption of agriculture took place within the context of the decreasing edible productivity associated with changes in vegetation and sea levels (1976: 476–8).

Michael Jochim (1976) constructed a model of the subsistence and settlement patterns of Mesolithic hunter-gatherers in south-western Germany, based on cross-cultural ethnographic research. Assuming that such hunter-gatherers were rational decision-makers, he focused on three interrelated areas of study: the resource use schedule (e.g. the density, mobility and yields of local plant and animal resources), site placement (e.g. in relation to distances to procure these resources) and demographic arrangements (e.g. the potential for population aggregation during the year). The ecological model enabled Jochim (1976: 141–3) to make predictions of the location, the months occupied, group size and the dietary importance of different animal resources of Mesolithic sites in his study area and comparison of these predictions (1976: 145–86) with regions and archaeologically known sites. In a later expansion of this ecological approach, Jochim (1981) presented a more general, cross-cultural model of the behaviour that was practised by human societies through four 'strategies for survival': feeding strategies (e.g. how much of different resources to be exploited), procurement strategies (the efficiency of different technologies, the organisation of human labour), settlement strategies (permanence, location, size and composition of settlements) and maintenance strategies (e.g. territoriality, storage and population control used as responses to imbalances between demand and resources).

BOX 3.2 BIOGEOGRAPHY AND
MEDITERRANEAN ISLANDS

John Cherry used the theory of island biogeography as 'a useful exploratory strategy in modelling the ways in which insularity ... (affected) ... the distribution and adaptation of humans, as well as other animals' in the Mediterranean Basin (1990: 146). His two starting points (1981: 49) were the 'distance effect' (the arrival of colonists, including humans, at a quicker rate on islands located closer to the mainland) and the 'area effect' (small islands that have less ecological variation have lower species diversity and sizes and therefore higher rates of extinction). Rates of colonisation increase where there are 'stepping-stones', or clusters, of islands. Given these biogeographical principles, Cherry (1981: 49–52) selected island size and remoteness as his key measures of the relative dating and probability of successful human colonisation of Mediterranean islands. For the East Mediterranean (1981: 52–6) he claims 'some confirmation of the predicted pattern' for larger islands, closer to the mainland, being colonised earlier than smaller and more remote islands, although there were notable anomalies. In contrast, such patterning was much less clear in the West Mediterranean (1981: 56–8). Rather than colonisation of each island being a single episode, he argued for 'many tentative, impermanent, short-distance reciprocal movements by mere handfuls of individuals' (1981: 60), subject to the risks of unsuccessful colonisation ('extinction') on small and ecologically less variable islands. In addition to the more rapid expansion of agricultural groups onto West Mediterranean islands, Cherry proposed that the large islands of Sicily, Corsica and Sardinia acted as 'mini-mainlands' (1981: 63) in facilitating this rapidity and successful colonisation.

In a later publication, Cherry (1990; see also Broodbank 2006) updated the details of colonisation of Mediterranean islands and refined his model of the colonisation process, for example distinguishing short-term/seasonal human presence (accidental/ unsuccessful?) from permanent occupation. Human colonisation also coincided over time with extinction of endemic species on the Balearic islands, Corsica and Cyprus, in line with the biogeographical principle that the number of an island's species is a balance between the arrival of new species and the extinction of existing species.

Is the theory of island biogeography an example of environmental determinism? Does a theory based on the natural world fail to help us study and understand the cultural world? Its defenders would argue that human communities play an active role in the colonisation process, the success or failure of which requires networks of social interaction, as well as the choice of ultimately successful subsistence practices, in new environments (e.g. resource diversification). Biogeographical principles guide us towards a study of the archaeological record produced by colonisers, who are both biological and cultural beings. The extent of insularity after initial colonisation in areas like the Mediterranean, of island people being cut off from communities on other islands or mainlands, is increasingly a cultural rather than a natural matter, as islanders become the products of their own created history and the island ecosystems became increasingly the products of human action. Ultimately, the specific environments in which human communities colonised islands were perceived through their culture, but there had to be sufficient 'tie-up' between perceived and actual environments for these communities to continue to exist.

HUMAN BEHAVIOURAL ECOLOGY

Ecosystems approaches used within processual archaeology developed from the late 1970s into what was to become known as **human behavioural ecology** (HBE). This branch of evolutionary ecology focuses on (a bit of mouthful!) 'the function of behavioral patterns in terms of their immediate, contextually contingent adaptive value to individuals', in other words 'what is the current, adaptive fitness-related role of behavior x in a subject's life?' (Bird and O'Connell 2012: 38). In Darwinian terms, this adaptive function of human behaviour is given preference over its inheritance: 'at issue is not how behavior is learned or transmitted between individuals, but how behavior functions in ways that promote specific adaptive goals of individuals' (2012: 38). The behaviour of these individuals (e.g. their subsistence) is shaped by ecological constraints and centres on rational strategies that calculate the costs and benefits of different course of action. For example, what are the costs and benefits of hunting particular animal species or cultivating different plant species and how do they enable human beings to adapt to their environments? To see how these questions are answered, let us look at two bodies of theory used in HBE, namely **optimal foraging theory** and **signalling theory**. For the benefit of simplicity, note that early examples of HBE do not consider how human beings modify their own environments and those of other organisms. This is addressed by another approach, **niche construction theory**, which shows (among other things) how what are argued to be the best courses of action in human feeding strategies change with the modified physical environments (Shennan 2012: 30–1).

Optimal Foraging Theory

Optimal foraging theory (OFT, or just 'foraging theory') 'is a set of models designed to address questions about variability in resource acquisition, time allocation and the spatial organisation of foraging strategies' (Bird and O'Connell 2012: 42–3). Foraging for food requires decisions about which animal and plant species to exploit, where and when to exploit them, how long to exploit the same species and the balance of species in the diet in the habitats in which they live, and what to do when specific resources begin to decline in frequency and availability. As with other animal species, human foragers (whether hunter-gatherers or agriculturalists) have to allocate time and energy to the search for, and pursuit of, their prey, as well as to the transport and processing of that prey. Do you consume hunted animals where you kill them? Butcher them and take them back to your settlement? How do you cook them (e.g. boiling, roasting) given the technologies you have available? Although basic to human existence, such foraging for food is one activity, alongside a range of social practices and interactions, to which individuals and communities have to allocate time and labour.

Why 'optimal' foraging theory? The answer lies in the assumption of 'optimisation': foragers will wish to optimise the benefits they get from the acquisition of resources given the time and energy costs they invest in such activities. 'In the long run, natural selection is expected to favor foragers that maximise their rate of energy capture' (Nagaoka 2002: 421). Those individuals who are closer to optimising their foraging activities will have the better adapted behaviour to pass on culturally to their offspring, what is in Darwinian terms called their adaptive 'fitness'.

How is OFT put into practice? The first step is to propose models of how the types and ranges of foods are chosen for inclusion in what is called an 'optimal diet'. How much time and energy is spent in locating, pursuing and processing prey in relation to the energy gained in prey consumption? Where is foraging best pursued in the landscape ('the optimal foraging space') to enable the capture and consumption of the optimal diet? How does the organisation of foragers in different-sized groups increase the efficiency of their foraging and ultimately their adaptiveness through practices such as the organisation of labour and the sharing of food? The most basic of these models are those of 'diet breadth' and 'patch choice' (Box 3.3), which have been argued to work well as predictions of animal behaviour. The extent to which these models could predict human foraging strategies initially focused on hunter-gatherer case studies using ethnographic (and later archaeological) data (Box 3.4). In each case, the usefulness of the OFT models was evaluated by the degree of fit between their predictions of subsistence practices or change and the observations made on the ethnographic and archaeological data.

BOX 3.3 DIET BREADTH AND PATCH CHOICE MODELS

When foragers are out looking for food, do they pursue any and all animals, and collect any and all plants that they encounter? Do they make decisions on the basis of the availability and density of these species (e.g. herds as opposed to individual animals, dense stands of wild cereals)? According to the diet breadth model, foragers rank their prey according to the amount of energy they provide per unit of time in relation to the energy the foragers expend in pursuing, capturing/collection and processing them: the greater this return and the higher the combined prey ranking, the more efficient it is to exploit them. If foragers wish to add new resources to their diets, they will choose the next highest-ranking ones. This strategy explains why some widely available resources may not be exploited. It follows that over-exploitation of particular resources and their decreasing return rates leads to an increasing number of foraged resources (diet breadth) in the diet.

But is this the whole story? Other factors such as technological changes can have a decisive impact on the range of exploited resources and on the exploitation of new resources. As important is the recognition that animal and plant resources are not necessarily distributed evenly in the landscape. Often they occur in patches (hence the patch choice model) and foragers have to select which patches to exploit, and for how long a period of time, to produce their optimal diet, especially under conditions of depletion in the quantity and predictability of specific resources. This model predicts that a patch will be abandoned when its returns are less than those for the total environment exploited by the foragers.

BOX 3.4 ARCHAEOLOGICAL APPLICATIONS OF OPTIMAL FORAGING THEORY

Winterhalder and Smith (1981) published the initial collection of ethnographic and archaeological uses of OFT. More recent, excellently presented introductions to both kinds of uses are given by Shennan (2002: 142–76) and Bird and O'Connell (2012: 42–52). As Shennan (2002: 148–9) points out, we cannot observe (without time travel) the behaviour of prehistoric foragers and must often rely on animal bone assemblages (with their better preservation than plant food assemblages) as indicators of resource ranking and diet breadth. On the other hand, the reconstruction of changing palaeoenvironments supports inferences of long-term changes in resource exploitation.

For an instructive example of OFT in action, let us consider Nagaoka's (2002) study of a widely observed change in foraging practices before white colonisation in New Zealand. Between AD 1250 and 1400, the intensive exploitation of species of flightless birds ('moas') was succeeded in midden deposits by foraging of fish, shellfish and small birds. For one particular midden, the Shag

River Mouth site, Nagaoka re-analyses the large faunal assemblage against the predictions of OFT. This makes interesting reading as an archaeological study (e.g. using the body size of exploited animals as a proxy measure of their ranking, integrating environmental change into the definition of patches, showing how technological change lowered the costs of the capture and hence the ranking of animals). Early in the midden sequence, exploitation centred on inland and coastal patches, with specialised exploitation of the moas. In line with OFT predictions, as moa availability declined in the inland patches, lower ranked and previously unexploited species increased in the diet. The same patterns occurred on the coast, although with much broader resource exploitation, while the use of offshore patches increased. Settlement patterns and population mobility also changed in line with these foraging patterns.

Like all Darwinian archaeologies, the application of OFT to human behaviour has been criticised and debated. For example, the exploitation of animals and plants is for non-food uses as well as for consumption (what about the time and energy costs of making baskets, nets, cord, etc.?), and cultural taboos play roles in decisions on whether or not to exploit particular animal species. What about the non-optimal behaviour practised by both hunter–gatherers and agriculturalists? And are we justified in using theories that have their origins in the market economics of capitalist societies (individuals making rational decisions on the costs and benefits of particular actions)?

SIGNALING THEORY

The approaches so far grouped together under the heading of HBE share an emphasis on rational decision-making when studying 'such components of adaptive success as food acquisition, mate choice and resource competition' (Bliege Bird and Smith 2005: 221). In contrast signaling theory attempts to integrate what has been described as 'irrational', 'altruistic' or 'wasteful' examples of behaviour into adaptationist research on human societies. Such behaviour includes the construction of monumental architecture, aspects of religious activities, competitive feasting, the production and circulation of nonutilitarian objects, 'prestige' hunting, warfare and artistic traditions, all of which have time and energy costs in terms of human labour. They are normally studied as examples of social and symbolic behaviour, human rather than animal practices, and usually grouped in archaeology under headings such as 'symbolic and structural', or 'social' archaeology.

Such forms of 'irrational' behaviour have been noted by social theorists since the end of the nineteenth century (Bliege Bird and Smith 2005: 222–3). For example, there is now a long tradition in anthropology of studying precapitalist societies that invest time and labour in the competitive giving and destruction of various material items, from feathers to food: the more giving and destruction of such 'costly' (and hence valued) items (for example, in the large-scale feasts of indigenous tribes on the northwest coast of North America), the greater the social 'prestige' of the individuals engaging in these activities. What appears to be 'irrational' and 'wasteful' behaviour has social rewards. While 'rational' social practices had adaptive advantages for human populations, such examples of 'irrational' behaviour were decidedly non-adaptive and marginal to human survival.

Signaling theory proposes that 'costly displays successfully transmit information that is vital to establishing and maintaining relationships, especially in large-scale complex social environments' (Galle 2010: 21). The individuals who engage in these 'displays' (e.g. building monuments, giving feasts) have conflicting interests (e.g. competing for positions of leadership) and gain mutually by clearly and visibly 'signaling' these interests to each other. 'Costly signaling theory attempts to explain how seemingly inefficient (or costly) types of behavior can evolve through natural selection, as long as these behaviors communicate a series of underlying qualities that are of interest to observers' (McGuire and Hildebrandt 2005: 698). 'Benefits ... to interacting include recognition of social status, entrees into successful economic partnerships, a long-term social alliance, or the discovery of a well-matched mate' (Galle 2010: 21). If you organise a large, public feast, this is a 'costly' activity in terms of time and energy. If you hunt larger prey, this can also be costly, as the time, energy and risks involved may make the yield of meat (and hence calories and protein) less efficient than for some smaller species of animals. But the display of hunting skills helps hunters to 'gain social recognition and, compared to non-hunters, begin reproduction at an earlier age, have higher age-specific reproductive success, obtain higher quality mates…and average a higher frequency of mates and other co-resident sexual partners' (McGuire and Hildebrandt 2005: 699). This is the evolutionary pay-off of such behaviour by humans.

Whether signaling theory is applied to the biological or the social sciences, its practitioners claim that it provides a unifying theory (Bliege Bird and Smith 2005: 221) for attempts to understand how the interaction of communication and status (or 'prestige') is important to the evolution of animals and humans. A range of informative examples taken from anthropology are presented by Bliege Bird and Smith (2005) and Bird and O'Connell (2006), while Roscoe (2009) argues that small-scale societies in contact-era Highland New Guinea engaged in symbolic (or 'ritualised') fighting that 'reliably communicated who would win a fight to the death without anyone having to engage in an actual fight to the death' (2009: 90) and thereby 'managed their conflicts of interest' (2009: 71): social structure as a whole and collaborative action were maintained and not ripped apart by physical warfare, while various individuals and subgroups who 'honestly signal qualities (fighting ability, industriousness, management skills, etc.) that make them both valued allies and mates and also formidable competitors' (2009: 102) gained in ways (such as positions of leadership) that did not threaten this social structure. Archaeological applications of signaling theory are less well developed, given that they have only been produced during the last two decades (Box 3.5).

Criticisms of the application of signaling theory in archaeology have centred on the assumptions of the theory itself and its articulation with the specific empirical record under study. Does the theory unify the biological and social sciences, or does it reduce understandings of the archaeological past to those of behavioural ecology? In the context of feasting behaviour, Hayden (2014: 56–7) contends that a focus on this as an example of a 'wasteful' activity that gives producers (i.e. the preparers and givers of feasts) a selective advantage over non-producers overstates the case, and that 'to limit the motivations and purposes of feasts to these factors is far too narrow a view of why people give feasts'. Whatever the contexts of its application in archaeology, does not signaling theory result in a static understanding of the past?

BOX 3.5 SIGNALING THEORY AND PRESTIGE HUNTING

During the Middle Archaic period (c. 2000 BC–AD 1000) of California and across the western Great Basin of North America, archaeologists have noted a marked and consistent rise in big-game hunting. McGuire and Hildebrandt (2005) have documented this change in the western Great Basin from their excavations at Pie Creek Shelter in comparison with earlier excavations at Gatecliff Shelter. Why did this change occur? McGuire and Hildebrandt reject changes in the productivity of, and group adaptation to, the environment as being the cause of this shift to big-game exploitation. Instead, they note the concurrent intensification of plant exploitation (from plant remains at Pie Creek Shelter and grinding stone frequencies at Gatecliff Shelter) and infer the development of 'two very different subsistence regimes (i.e. male large-game hunting and female intensive plant procurement and processing)' (2005: 703). 'Middle Archaic men and women were engaged in wholly different foraging agendas, one logistically oriented, highly mobile, and potentially suboptimal with regard to energetic returns; the other more residential, less mobile, and sensitive to provisioning efficiency' (2005: 703–4). This inference of a gendered division of labour is supported by differences in settlement organisation and osteoarthritis frequencies across the western Great Basin. At the same time, there was what is called 'a fluorescence of artistic elaboration in material culture and rock art' symbolising both male hunting and female provisioning of plant foods. Using signaling theory, McGuire and Hildebrandt interpret the increase in exploitation of large game as male 'prestige hunting', a means for them to advance social position through symbolic communication (e.g. 'I am a better hunter than he is, therefore I merit greater social value'), and to play a greater role in group decision-making, and enjoy greater reproductive success through the attraction of female mates.

TRANSMISSION AND CULTURAL EVOLUTION

If biological evolution works by variation, selection and transmission of genes, then how does cultural evolution work? Evolutionary archaeology as advocated by Dunnell and a tradition of research over the last four decades dismisses the classification of human societies into successive stages, as seen in the mid-nineteenth and mid-twentieth centuries (see above). Instead, the focus is on the behaviour of individual human beings that is embodied in, and practised through, culture and transmitted from one generation to another. Do specific artefacts have reproductive advantages (e.g. stone tool types in relation to the colonisation of new habitats)? Can we distinguish, as Dunnell (1978) suggested, between functional as opposed to stylistic traits (the latter changing by chance rather than selection)? How can we, as archaeologists, study artefacts and cultural traditions using the concepts of variation, transmission and selection taken from biological evolution? Are the principles of biological and cultural evolution the same?

The use of the concepts of variation, adaptation and selection in archaeology has been discussed above, so we will now focus on transmission. The starting point is the influential work of evolutionary ecologists Robert Boyd and Peter Richerson (1985) and their **dual inheritance theory** (also called 'Co-evolutionary Theory'). Culture (see also Chapter 4), as they define it (1985: 2), is a system of information ('knowledge, values and other factors that influence behaviour') that is shared in cultural traditions and transmitted by social learning (teaching and imitation) between generations. The role of culture and social learning in this transmission, primarily from parent to offspring, is much greater in the adaptations of human cultures than it is in those of other animal species (Shennan 2002: 38). Examples of changes in culture include intentional innovation (e.g. production of new types of bronze weapons to meet needs of change in warfare behaviour) and copying errors in artefact production (e.g. in hand-made pottery form and decoration), the latter process being analogous to genetic mutation. This transmission of information, like genetic inheritance, serves an adaptive purpose, generating and passing on variation that will be acted on by selection. However, cultural transmission is not the same as genetic transmission (see Boyd and Richerson (1985) for specifically cultural mechanisms of transmission). Shennan (2002: 64) points out that 'successful responses to selective pressures on cultural traditions will not necessarily produce outcomes enhancing the survival and reproductive success of individuals in the population concerned'. Social learning applies specifically to culture and cultural evolution. Cultural information can be passed between generations ('vertical transmission') and, unlike the transmission of genes, between unrelated people ('horizontal transmission'). Social learning and cultural transmission lead to a faster pace of change than genetic evolution.

The most accessible, introductory account of the archaeological study of cultural traditions and their transmission is given by Shennan (2002: 66–99). He proposes that there are cultural analogues to biological processes (e.g. compare the copying errors in pottery production mentioned above to genetic mutations), but also (following Boyd and Richerson's model) mechanisms of change specific to cultural traditions. These mechanisms include changing forms of behaviour as a result of calculations of its costs and benefits in relation to different ways of doing things. As Shennan points out (2002: 64), cultural and genetic transmission 'lead to the production of heritable variation and its modification through time'. Defining cultural traditions is, of course, a long-standing archaeological concern. We have been analysing variation in artefacts, and arranging them into types and evolutionary sequences since the mid-nineteenth century, and defining past cultures in time and space since the late nineteenth and early twentieth centuries. This focus on typologies, cultures and 'influences' between different cultures was roundly criticised in processual archaeology, with its focus on culture as an adaptive system (see above Chapter 1). Shennan uses Boyd and Richerson's dual inheritance theory to propose four areas of study for a Darwinian approach to cultural traditions:

1. The establishment of reliable methods for constructing cultural traditions (or 'lineages') 'linked by historical continuity based on the transmission of information through time' (2002: 73–8).
2. The study of the extent to which coherent cultures of varying sizes can be defined in space and time (2002: 78–83).
3. The study of how these cultural traditions originated. How far, and why, did they have clearly defined and maintained boundaries (2002: 83–91)?
4. How far do artefact forms and cultural 'packages' tie in with specific languages and genetic groups (2002: 91–9)?

Clear examples of archaeological case studies are presented in relation to each area of study and are worth careful reading. Eerkens and Lipo (2005) argue that the generation of variation in tiny copying errors in artefacts, and the amount of such variation through time, can relate to different kinds of cultural transmission. Their analysis of selected traits of Owens Valley (California) projectile points and Woodland period (Illinois) pottery sherds shows how simple copying errors may (in the case of the former) or may not (in the case of the latter) fully account for this variation. The transmission of craft skills through both horizontal and vertical transmission is also attracting more interest (Box 3.6).

BOX 3.6 MODES OF TRANSMISSION AND CRAFT SKILLS

Hosfield (2009: 46) defines craft skills as 'those motor and cognitive skills required for the production of end products through the manipulation of raw materials by the use of tools, including the human hand', the products themselves ranging from stone tools and pottery through to metalworking. How are these skills acquired? How is knowledge of skills and the desired products transmitted? Do different modes of transmission have implications for degrees of innovation and conservatism seen in these products? As an important step towards answering such questions, Hosfield has assembled a cross-cultural ethnographic and ethno-archaeological database of 72 case studies providing a range of information on the mode of cultural transmission, the nature of the craft skills and of the material culture patterning (e.g. types, designs, technologies). Keeping in mind the limitations of the data, a statistical analysis of the relationships between these variables showed a significant association between, on the one hand, vertical transmission of skills from parents and conservatism in material culture, and on the other hand between horizontal modes of transmission and innovation. At the same time, there was evidence that factors other than modes of transmission contributed to this conservatism and innovation. Hosfield (2009: 56) concludes by suggesting some ways in which archaeologists can use these insights in their studies of material culture patterning (e.g. 'an index of connectivity for a particular archaeological community/region/culture could reveal relationships with the relative conservatism/innovation observed over time in the craft skills' material record(s)').

EVOLUTIONARY PSYCHOLOGY

Ultimately, the transmission of culture works through the thoughts and actions of people. We perceive the world around us through our senses and our consciousness. We are social beings and we communicate with each other, both through language and the material world that we have created. Smartphones and laptops give us means to communicate directly via speech and text messages in ways that were previously unimaginable. Such objects, as well as clothing, houses, motor cars and so on, are also used to symbolise things about ourselves and our place in the social order. The use of our creativity to produce this material world makes us unlike other animal species.

This use of the human mind makes it an important area for study. How does the human mind work and how has it evolved? How, why and when did human characteristics such as language, music, religion and art develop? These are big questions. For some archae-ologists, they are at the limits of the inferences we can make with any reliability from our material evidence. Such pessimism has been challenged, with varying degrees of success and intensity. Since the 1980s what is called 'cognitive' or 'cognitive-processual' archaeology has addressed 'the study of ways of thought as inferred from mate-rial remains' (Renfrew 1994: 3) and tries to make those inferences of past human cognition and symbolism as well-founded as possible (Renfrew 2012). Since the 1990s, an array of theoretical approaches drawn from the cognitive sciences has invigorated archaeological research on the 'big questions' of the nature and evolution of the human mind (Mithen 1998, 2001). These approaches are drawn, for example, from linguistics, neuroscience, evolutionary anthropol-ogy, developmental psychology and evolutionary psychology. Let us focus on the last of these.

Evolutionary psychology proposes that 'human cognitive and behavioural tendencies evolved during the Plio-Pleistocene and (that) we can explain behaviour since that point as the product of past evolutionary changes' (Bentley et al. 2008: 120). Although this proposition was developed without engagement with archae-ological research, it has provided a stimulus for that research. For example, the evolutionary psychologists Cosmides and Tooby have argued that 'the modern human mind is constituted by a series of mental modules, each "designed" by natural selection to solve one specific adaptive problem that hunter-gatherers faced in the Pleistocene – problems such as choosing mates, finding food, and avoiding danger' (Mithen 2001: 101). Examples of mental modules include ones for tool-use, social exchange, child-care, friendship and grammar acquisition, all 'hard-wired' into all children's minds in all cultures at birth. But is this model of the human mind and its evolution convincing? Are the modules all appropriate for what the modern human mind does (Mithen 1998: 46ff)? Do they all operate exclusively of each other? The answers to these critical questions, coupled with the research of developmental psychologists and the material record of human evolution led Mithen (1998: 69) to propose three phases for the evolution of the mind, during which its different parts became more complexly linked to each other:

'**Phase 1**. Minds dominated by a domain of general intelligence – a suite of general-purpose learning and decision-making rules.
Phase 2. Minds in which general intelligence has been supplemented by multiple specialised intelligences, each devoted to a specific domain of behaviour, and each working in isolation from the others.
Phase 3. Minds in which the multiple specialised intelligences appear to be working together, with a flow of information and ideas between behavioural domains.'

These hypothetical phases are then traced through human evolution from the evidence we have for such features as tool-making, the development of language and religion: as the mind became more integrated, so major changes in human behaviour developed more rapidly (e.g. art in the Upper Palaeolithic).

Others (e.g. Dunbar *et al.* 2007) wrestle with the nature and evolution of culture, language and religion in terms of their capacities for transmitting behaviour and knowledge, and enhancing social cohesion. Archaeologists have also picked up on evolutionary psychologists' ideas about possible 'innate' human abilities (the outcome of natural selection in the Pleistocene) such as altruism and aspirations for status.

BONES OF CONTENTION

Not for nothing are the theories presented in this chapter referred to as being used in Darwinian archaeologies. They are also an introductory selection (see Shennan 2002 for a wide range of examples on themes including relations between populations and the resources they exploited, and the evolution of inequality and the ownership of property). Darwinian archaeologists disagree about the relative strengths and weaknesses of these approaches (e.g. the importance of adaptation, selection and transmission? how rapid cultural change can be understood?). For some it is Darwinian evolutionary theory that is the sole basis for an intellectually sound archaeological theory, explaining biology and culture: these are what Pluciennik (2011: 40) calls 'the evangelical extremes of the selectionist field'.

Do Darwinian archaeologies explain everything, both biology and culture? Do they reduce our material world, our behaviour, symbolism and our ideas to biology? What roles do social and ideological factors play in human choice and action over different scales of time and space? We may legitimately ask about the nature of differences between cultural and biological evolution. McGuire (2002: 129) argues that human beings, unlike other animals, are products and creators of history and that 'scholars are ill-advised to reduce our understanding of human action and social change to biological principles created for the study of other animals'; as such, Darwinian archaeologies are determinist and reductionist. According to this line of argument, human history is a record of our divergence from other animal species through culture, consciousness, intentionality, language, symbolism, creativity, the development of social institutions and history making. Human beings are not just another species. Could it be that Darwinian approaches have more to offer in the study of pre-modern than modern humans (Kristiansen 2004)? And to claim that Darwinian evolutionary theory is a theory of everything or the unifying theory between the biological and social sciences (see signaling theory above) is highly ambitious. If it were, then the next chapter would not be necessary! It is time to move back to social theories, especially those that have played a significant role in archaeology since the 1980s.

SUMMARY

- Ideas about cultural and biological evolution, and their relative importance, have fluctuated in popularity within the social sciences (including archaeology) and the natural sciences in the last two centuries. Evolutionary approaches to culture and society preceded those of biology. Darwin's theory of evolution supported the idea of a long time-span for human evolution, but was also used in a deterministic way in archaeology and popular culture in the late nineteenth century to legitimise social and political hierarchies.

- The study of cultural evolution was sidelined from the late nineteenth to the mid-twentieth centuries, although archaeology was one of a number of disciplines that continued to work on relationships between culture and nature using the Darwinian concept of adaptation.

- Cultural evolution played a major role in processual archaeology with the use of cross-cultural ethnographic analogies to study the evolution of types of society such as the chiefdom. Although fiercely debated and criticised, a tradition of cultural evolution continues to be present in archaeology.

- Alongside Marxism, Darwinian thought became more popular in archaeology from the late 1970s. It has focused on variation, adaptation, selection and transmission of cultural traditions. Rather than Darwinian archaeology, there is a group of Darwinian archaeologies: ecosystems research, human behavioural ecology (optimal foraging theory, signaling theory), cultural transmission (dual inheritance theory) and evolutionary psychology. In otherwise words, this is not a unified body of thought.

- Darwinian archaeologists disagree about the relative strengths and weaknesses of their approaches. Other archaeologists criticise these approaches as a whole for their perceived reduction of the study of culture to biology and for not focusing attention on the differences between cultural and biological evolution. They also criticise those Darwinians who argue that their theory is a unifying theory for all of archaeology, let alone the social and biological sciences. These debates continue.

FURTHER READING GUIDE

Johnson (2020) devotes one chapter each to cultural evolution and Darwinian evolution in archaeology, while Chapman (2003: 33–100) debates neo-evolutionism and other approaches to cultural change. Shennan (2002, 2012) gives the best and most comprehensive introductions to Darwinian archaeologies, while Shennan (2018) offers an ambitious and provocative use of evolutionary approaches linking the culture, demography and subsistence practices involved in the spread of farming from south-west Asia through Europe. Leppard and Fitzpatrick (2021) present a detailed introduction (with copious references) to the study of island colonisation in the Mediterranean (and its stimulus from island archaeology in the Pacific). Bird and O'Connell (2012) focus on Human Behavioural Ecology, including optimal foraging theory and signaling theory. The edited book by Winterhalder and Smith (1981) remains an important introduction to optimal foraging theory. Connolly (2017) introduces signaling theory and an accompanying collection of archaeological examples. A range of case studies on cultural transmission is given in Shennan (2002). An accessible introduction to evolutionary psychology is given by Dunbar *et al.* (2007). The papers in Renfrew and Zubrow (1994), along with Renfrew (2012) will give you a grasp of the field of 'cognitive archaeology', while the best guide to cognitive evolution remains Mithen's (1998) book and his short (2001) paper. Gamble *et al.* (2014) present a more recent study of the 'big problems' of the evolution of the human mind, social worlds, language, art and music. The most recent and informative presentation of evolutionary theory in archaeology is given by Prentiss (2021).

4

CULTURE, AGENCY AND IDENTITY

In the previous chapters, there has been much mention of culture and material culture, as well as society, social structure and social relations. But what exactly are 'culture' and 'material culture'? Do the objects that we study, whether above or below ground, whole or fragmentary, simply serve functional purposes? What about their symbolism and meanings? How are such meanings conveyed, how is culture transmitted and how does it change? What is the relationship between social structures and our actions and identities as individuals? Archaeologists have drawn upon a variety of high-level theories to try and answer these kinds of questions. But first, we need to put these theories along with those discussed in Chapters 2 and 3, into two broader intellectual contexts.

MODERNITY

The theoretical traditions of thinkers such as Marx, Weber, Durkheim and Darwin, as seen in Chapters 2 and 3, are grouped together in the social sciences as expressions of **modernity**, that is a way of thinking aimed at knowing the world around us through reason and scientific methods, which together have provided the basis for our understanding of human history. The eighteenth and nineteenth centuries were the high points of modernity, witnessing the growth of science, the development of capitalism, industrialisation and modern nation states, and the expansion of Western empires. Thomas (2004) shows how scientific knowledge of the world around us, coupled with the growth of reason as a means to understanding the human condition, had important consequences. It empowered a belief in our ability to

DOI: 10.4324/9781315657097-4

improve our world (progress), thus favouring ideas of the evolution of human societies through distinctive stages (see Chapter 3), to civilisation in the modern, Western world. Our reason was the product of our minds, which in turn were separate from our bodies (hence 'mind over matter'), in the same way that humans were subjects and the material world contained humanly produced objects. This was a division, like that between culture and nature, that has only been strongly challenged in recent decades (see Chapter 5). Archaeology's emergence as a distinctive practice was enabled by modernity.

POSTMODERNISM

Since the late 1960s, the key assumptions and approaches of modernity in a variety of disciplines (e.g. art, architecture, literary criticism) have been increasingly challenged by **postmodernism** (or the 'postmodern condition'). As with all intellectual movements that begin with the word 'post', it is often easier to agree on what postmodernism is a reaction to, rather than define in any agreed way what it actually is. Postmodernists have been compared to 'members of a loosely constituted and quarrelsome political party' (Butler 2002: 2). Among key exponents in Europe were Jean-Francois Lyotard, Jean Baudrillard, Jacques Lacan, Julia Kristeva, Jacques Derrida and Michel Foucault.

Postmodernists critiqued the concepts of rationality and progress, the existence of universal truths, the extent to which reality was discovered or constructed by us and seen through the language that we use, and the existence of testable ideas as opposed to 'stories' or 'narratives' about history. In place of these modernist concepts and ways of understanding the human condition, postmodernists saw 'truth' in relation to their intellectual and individual standpoints, and 'reality' as seen through the light of elite, ideological 'agendas' (Butler 2002: 16, 38). The French philosopher Michel Foucault placed emphasis on the relationship between scientific knowledge and power, rather than on objective truth. How do we arrive at knowledge of the world around us? For postmodernists, this knowledge is 'culturally conditioned and often politically motivated' (Orser 2015: 23). Thinkers needed to be self-conscious and self-critical ('reflexive') about their own cultural and political standpoints and how they shaped their knowledge of the world. Postmodernists also expressed disbelief towards what Jean-Francois Lyotard called 'metanarratives' (also called 'grand narratives') which 'are contained in or implied by major philosophies, such as Kantianism, Hegelianism and Marxism, which argue that history is progressive, that knowledge can liberate us, and that all knowledge has a secret unity' (Butler 2002: 13). Interestingly, these 'grand narratives' included what was called the Marxist 'Utopia' (that is, the socialist society ultimately produced by proletarian revolution against capitalism): as Butler (2002: 114) puts it 'postmodernists are by and large pessimists, many of them haunted by (their) lost Marxist revolutionary hopes'.

Postmodernism has also been widely criticised. Callinicos (1989: 3) argues that it denies 'any general pattern on which to base our conception of a true theory or a just society' and that postmodernists face a contradiction 'in using the tools of rationality – philosophical argument and historical analysis – in order to carry out the critique of reason as such' (1989: 26). Others, most notably Sokal and Bricmont (1998), have argued that postmodernism's critique of science is fundamentally flawed.

Postmodernism enjoyed a heyday of at least two decades in which its ideas and challenges permeated the social sciences and played an influential role in the development of postprocessual archaeology. Alongside critiques of archaeology as science and the use of the scientific method, including flirtations with **relativism** (are all interpretations of the past equally valid?), there have been debates on the extent to which our social, political and cultural 'standpoints' (see Box 1.3) impact on our interpretations of the past, and the ways in which archaeologists can open up to, and work with, indigenous peoples or other marginalised groups of people (Box 4.1). If there is any truth in our knowledge of the past, then, how do we evaluate competing interpretations of the past between such groups and archaeologists?

BOX 4.1 STANDPOINTS AND MULTIPLE NARRATIVES

White Western archaeologists have a long history of active research on the pasts of non-Western, indigenous societies. These archaeologists brought with them views of indigenous societies as representative of the earlier stages of cultural evolution, inferior in every way to their imperial overlords. These societies were regarded as static, without the characteristics of 'civilisation' (e.g. large monuments, urban centres, writing). In sub-Saharan Africa, 'early African peoples apparently did nothing else but make tools and search for food', having 'no social life and no social thought' (Andah 1995: 152).

In today's world, there are more members of indigenous peoples who have been trained as archaeologists in both the Western world and in their own countries. One of the important growth areas of contemporary archaeology is this development and that of the collaboration of archaeologists with indigenous communities.

> True collaboration involves actions such as engaging with Native people from the outset of research so they are involved in forming research questions and topics; respecting cultural values and interests involved in designing and carrying out research; involving community members (students, elders, and others as interested) in grant writing, analysis, and dissemination of results; and providing funds and time to examine culturally appropriate methods of community education and stewardship of the knowledge produced.
>
> (Atalay 2008: 132, 2012)

The respect that Atalay cites is for indigenous interests and rights (how they benefit from archaeological research), and for indigenous ways of understanding and relating to their pasts (e.g. oral traditions, customs).

Although indigenous and non-indigenous groups are coming at the past from different standpoints, including attitudes towards the curation of human remains and artefacts, there are increasing numbers of examples showing how archaeological evidence and indigenous knowledge systems can be studied together as different lines of evidence on the past (e.g. Nicholas and Markey 2015). Within this indigenous knowledge is that of local ecologies, defined as 'the integrated principles, practices and beliefs that reveal and perpetuate the interconnectedness of people, animals, plants, natural objects, supernatural entities and environments' (2015: 291). This knowledge ranges from the medicinal properties of plants to the exploitation and management of resources. As Nicholas and Markey point out, there are examples of congruence and non-congruence between the indigenous knowledge and archaeological and historical evidence (2015: 291–8). They caution against automatically prioritising of archaeological evidence in cases of non-congruence: indigenous sources may serve as a catalyst that can 'push archaeologists towards unanticipated conclusions' (2015: 302), thereby stimulating new research and generating new questions.

CULTURE

Culture has been mentioned in previous chapters, with brief reference to its meaning(s). Putting aside the everyday use of the term to refer to 'civilised' behaviour (e.g. going to the opera, art galleries and museums and being members of the National Trust), there are a variety of definitions used in the literature of archaeology and the social sciences (Table 4.1). Some definitions stress human behavioural abilities or habits, while others focus on ideas, attitudes and values that are expressed in written texts, traditions, mythologies, rituals and objects. In culture history (see Chapter 1), the objects made, used and circulated were collectively seen as the expression of shared ideas, beliefs and ultimately peoples, while processual archaeologists viewed culture as the means by which people adapted to their environments, and postprocessual archaeologists searched for the 'meanings that people construct to make sense of their lives' (Gibbon 2014: 156). All definitions in Table 4.1 share the assumption that culture is learned socially rather than biologically transmitted from one generation to another.

The anthropologist Peter Metcalf (2005: 2) gives perhaps the best introductory definition: culture is 'all those things that are instilled in a child by elders and peers as he or she grows up, everything from table manners to religion'. These are 'taken-for-granted ways of behaving, the general understandings of the way things are' and we are more 'self-conscious' about culture when 'we have crossed some kind of cultural boundary' (2005: 19). This does, of course, assume that different cultures are internally uniform (e.g. are they divided by class or subcultures based on shared values, styles, etc.?),

Table 4.1 Some definitions of culture

'Learned modes of behaviour and its material manifestations, socially transmitted from one generation to the next and from one society or individual to another'

'Patterns of ideas that permeate human behaviour'

'Shared ideas and beliefs'

'A set of meanings that people construct to make sense of their lives'

'That complex whole which includes knowledge, belief, art, law, morals, custom and any other capabilities and habits acquired by man as a member of society'

'Socially transmitted patterns of behaviour characteristic of a particular social group'

'Man's extrasomatic means of adaptation to the external environment'

'The inscription in stories, rituals, customs, objects and practices of the meanings in circulation at a specific time and place'

---

that their boundaries are clearly and consistently marked (e.g. by 'material' culture) and that people do not readily adopt behaviours and understandings from outside their culture (e.g. as in our globalised world today). Metcalf's definition also omits other facts such as our built and ambient environment. There is also debate about the overlap between the concepts of 'culture' and ideology', as well as the distinction between 'culture' and 'nature', and even the need for the concept of culture itself (see Chapter 5). In spite of these complexities, Metcalf (2005: 157–8) argues that his general definition is widely held in anthropology, but that 'the concept of culture must be made to serve us, not to imprison us'.

MATERIAL CULTURE

If the definition of culture is debatable, then surely, we are on safer ground with that of **material culture**, a concept that has become central to interdisciplinary studies since the 1970s? There is even a *Journal of Material Culture,* as well as an established tradition of modern material culture studies. You might think that 'material culture' is another way of saying 'artefacts', produced in material form by us to fulfil basic needs such as chopping down trees, storing water and defending yourself against violent attacks. The extent to which human beings produce and make use of such artefacts creates material worlds beyond those of our nearest relatives, the non-human primates. By definition artefacts are *material* forms of culture: whereas culture is, according to Deetz (1996: 35), 'socially transmitted rules for behavior, ways of thinking and doing things', material culture is both a material product and part of culture. It is what Thomas (2007: 20) argues 'represents at once ideas that have been made material, and natural substance that has been rendered cultural'. Is the equation of material culture with artefacts sufficient, and what do we, as archaeologists, do with material culture? Why is it important to us?

During the processes of production (see Chapter 2), we transform perishable and non-perishable raw materials into material culture, from the smallest ornaments to the largest cathedrals and palaces. We create a material world and, as we shall see, we are created by it. As Deetz (1996: 35) put it, 'material culture is useful in emphasizing how profoundly our world is the product of our thoughts, as that sector of our physical environment that we modify through cultur-ally determined behavior'. Putting aside for now this opposition between mind (culture) and matter (material culture) (see Chapter 5), Deetz (1996: 35–6) even suggested that we should reach beyond artefacts and include such things as cuts of meat, domesticated livestock and ploughed fields as material culture, and that material culture does not have to be 'solid' (he used examples including hot-air balloons).

The study of material culture by archaeologists has character-ised the discipline's development since the nineteenth century. The types, styles and contexts of this evidence have been central to our construction of chronological and spatial frameworks, and our inference of past 'cultures' (what Gordon Childe defined as the material remains of past peoples) and past social, political and eco-nomic differences. Artefacts are studied in groups by functions and styles, as well as their contexts and sequences within the sites that we excavate.

Within processual archaeology, material culture enhanced human adaptation to the physical and human environment. Societies were normally in a state of equilibrium and only changed under the stim-ulus of external factors. Styles and distributions of material culture reflected human behaviour. For example, repeated patterns in the treatment of the dead (e.g. the forms of disposal, the artefacts placed within graves) were argued to 'reflect' social differences within and between societies.

But objects of all sorts are not there just to perform functions: biros enabling us to write, glasses helping the myopic to see more clearly, or clothing covering our embarrassment. In all these examples, the material culture symbolises something to us, it has meanings that are expressed and conveyed to other people. Think of the styles of clothing you wear, or the accessories you carry, and think about the reasons you buy them: are they fashionable or do they express religious, social or cultural affiliations? What meanings do they carry? Hodder's (1982a) ethnoarchaeological research in east Africa studied the symbolism of material objects and how this was expressed in people's daily lives. He argued that patterning in material culture may or may not express cultural differences. Such differences (e.g. on the boundaries between different cultures) exist but they are not always symbolised. From these studies, Hodder developed the argument that material culture does not 'reflect' human behaviour but 'can actively justify the actions and intentions of human groups' (1982a: 36). Symbolism can be 'manipulated' as part of social strategies. It has an 'active role' in daily life, hence the title of Hodder's book, *Symbols in Action*. 'Each use of an artefact through its previous associations and usage, has a significance and meaning within society so that the artefact is an active force in social change' (Hodder 1982b: 10). The meanings of material culture need to be studied in context. A dinner jacket may be thought suitable for a formal occasion but over the top for a pub crawl.

According to this argument, human intentions, beliefs, and attitudes, in other words, culture in Metcalf's definition, stand between social relations and their expression in material culture (Hodder 1982a: 211). A good example of this is the disposal of the dead, which did not 'reflect' in any direct or unambiguous way the structure or complexity of a living society: Hodder (1982c: 144) concluded that 'because of the dominant role of cultural codes and ideologies, the aspects of social organization which are represented in burial may be ideals picked out from practical social relations or even in contrast to them, reverting and distorting'. People are not directly conscious of these codes and ideologies. This was one of the reasons why archaeologists became interested in an influential body of theory derived from anthropology.

STRUCTURALISM

It is not surprising that attempts to make sense of variations in culture and what they might mean to human societies have looked for underlying, simple patterns and structures. Unlike Marxism's focus on structures such as the forces and relations of production in the material world, proponents of **structuralism** (in disciplines like linguistics, psychoanalysis and anthropology) in all its forms (Layton 1997:63–97; Gosden 1999:111–16; Hodder and Hutson 2003: 45–74) have sought to identify the unconscious rules, structures and beliefs in cultures that shape human actions. As Layton (1997: 74) puts it 'structuralist theory explains the structure of society as the product of ideas rather than the materialist conditions of existence'. For example, the famous French anthropologist Claude Lévi-Strauss argued that particular kinship systems and myths of unrelated societies in different continents were so closely similar as to reflect the existence of timeless, shared meanings and thought patterns, what he called 'deep structures'. Following the example of the early twentieth-century Swiss linguist Ferdinand de Saussure, he viewed culture, its rules and meanings, as working like a language, with its structures ('langue' in French) and speech ('parole'). In particular, he argued that the human mind divided and categorised the external world, or what we might call 'reality', in terms of a fairly limited range of universal 'binary' oppositions (e.g. male/female; culture/nature; inside/outside; life:/death; pure/impure) that distinguished different cultures.

A marked focus of structuralist approaches in anthropology from the 1960s was on the symbolic organisation of domestic space as shown in the layout of the individual structures and settlements, and the distribution of daily activities within them. For example, Levi-Strauss's (1963) study of houses and villages of the Bororo Indians in the Amazon Basin distinguished binary oppositions between male and female (as seen in the layout of a central men's house surrounded by family huts on the village edge) and sacred and profane (central ceremonial area vs. peripheral female domestic activities). Pierre Bourdieu's (1970) often-cited analysis of the Kabyle Berber house in Algeria found patterning that he ascribed to opposition between males (culture and light) and females (nature and darkness).

How does structuralism help us as archaeologists? How might we determine patterns in material culture and thereby identify the structures by which the mind categorised the external world? What does this tell us about how society is ordered? Analyses of pottery decoration have been used to determine design structures, focusing on symmetry analysis and how overall designs can be built up (or 'generated'), and of binary oppositions in the study of prehistoric rock art (e.g. Hodder and Hutson 2003: 47–59). Study of the structural organisation of settlements was practised by processual archaeologists to make inferences of social differences (e.g. Clarke 1972 on the Iron Age settlement of Glastonbury). These were analyses of structure but not using structuralism. In contrast, Parker Pearson (1996) explicitly used Levi-Strauss' and Pierre Bourdieu's work on the symbolic structure of household spaces as a basis for study of Late Bronze Age and Iron Age round houses in Britain. This kind of archaeological analysis has been pursued quite widely in studies of these periods, linking the order in the division of space within settlements and roundhouses to rules, structures and beliefs that exemplify the communities' understanding of the world around them.

While structuralist analyses of a range of archaeological evidence have served as essential bridges to inferences about symbolism and meaning in past societies, they have also been heavily criticised (e.g. Hodder and Hutson 2003: 59–65). Their basis in assumptions about timeless meanings and thought patterns across vast, unconnected distances reduces their value in terms of historical analysis. How and why do changes in symbolism take place? Structures, whether of the mind or in our relations to the material world (as in Marxism), do not change without human action (see Chapter 2 and below). Such criticisms began to be aired by anthropologists around the same time as the introduction of structuralism into archaeology in the early 1980s. Woodward and Hughes (2007) also to stressed the need for careful study of archaeological contexts (e.g. activity areas, foundation deposits or ritual abandonment practices) before ambitious and wide-ranging social and structural inferences.

Criticisms of structuralism in both anthropology and archaeology are certainly weighty and have been sufficient to decrease the popularity of this -ism. But they did not signify the end of the study of meaning through objects. The Swiss de Saussure and the American Charles Sanders Peirce (both of whom died immediately before WW1 with substantially unpublished work during their lifetimes) are together called founders of **semiotics**, the study of signs and what they stand for in the human world. Peirce's work is more challenging to understand but has attracted some attention in archaeology during the last two decades (e.g. Preucel 2006). Unlike de Saussure, he argued that the relationship between the two parts of a sign (the 'signifier', the word that is the sign, and the 'signified', the concept for which the word is used) is not arbitrary, and that the meaning of a word can be understood from a sign's context. If you substitute 'object' for 'word', the relevance for Peirce's work becomes clearer (see above, for the discussion of material culture). Whereas de Saussure was mainly focused on the structure of languages ('parole'), Peirce takes us more into the dynamic nature of signs and actual speech, a difference that parallels that between structure and agency (see below).

POSTSTRUCTURALISM

The roots of **poststructuralism** lay in both linguistics and philosophy, and emerged from critiques of structuralism that began within French postmodern thought in the 1960s and 1970s. Key individuals included Michel Foucault, Jacques Derrida, Roland Barthes and Giles Deleuze. Poststructuralism is defined generally as 'a theory, or a group of theories, concerning the relationship between human beings, the world, and the practice of making and reproducing meanings' (Belsey 2002:5). As in structuralism, poststructuralists argued that culture worked like a language. As Belsey (2002: 6) puts it, 'after food and shelter, which are necessary for survival, language and its symbolic analogues exercise the most crucial determinations in our social relations, our thought processes, and our understanding of who and what we are'. Language expresses and signifies (things, ideas), for example, through words, structures (e.g. grammar, syntax), symbols and images.

For poststructuralists, the analogy between culture and language focused on writing rather than speech. Culture was a text that we read and meaning is communicated through texts. At face value, this seems straightforward: authors write texts, the texts contain the meanings expressed by the author and the reader understands or absorbs those meanings. But the author writes in a particular language and its form and structure may make it difficult to convey his/her meaning when translated into another language. The meanings conveyed by the author (in whichever language he/she is writing) are shaped (consciously and unconsciously) by factors of education, class, gender, ethnicity, etc., as are the perspectives of the reader. Different readers may see different meanings in the same text, and these meanings may not coincide with those of the author. Readers are thus empowered and meanings can be manipulated. As the literary critic Roland Barthes argued, there is no definitive reading of a text and 'the birth of the reader must be at the cost of the death of the author'.

This is a gross simplification of the ideas expressed, often in challenging ways, by poststructuralists, who provided a less ahistorical approach than we see in structuralism, but it gives us a start and leads us to think about how this might be relevant to archaeology. Past people would have 'read' material culture, its various forms and styles, in making sense of the world around them. Our understanding, and that of 'social actors' (see below) in the past, of the material world, from portable artefacts through built structures to entire landscapes, requires close reading of the contexts in which such material culture exists. Changes in the forms and functions of material culture may emerge from different readings through time (see, for example, Hodder 1988 on the change from Neolithic enclosures in Western Europe with non-domestic and ritual to defended functions).

Does this amount to a poststructuralist archaeology? Although the case was made for treating material culture as a text, this was 'a very selective and watered-down tap of poststructuralism, a question of influence rather than explicit grounding' (Olsen 2010: 46–7). But is the language in a text an appropriate and useful analogy for the material culture that we study? As Hodder himself points out, in language there is an arbitrary relationship between meaning and how it is signified (e.g. different ways of symbolising wealth or maleness), whereas the same is not true of material culture: a good example is that of gold being of high value because of its long-lived and rare character. Gosden (1992: 807) also argues as follows: 'people and the world shape each other in mutual interaction: we shape the world and it alters us. In order to understand this interaction, we cannot retreat from the material world into a world of symbols. People's relationship to their material world is at least as strong as their relationship to language and is quite different'. Symbolism and meaning are important, but how do societies 'work' on a daily basis? Do human beings blindly and passively follow social structures? How is culture transmitted and how does it change?

STRUCTURE AND AGENCY

In Chapter 2, we saw how Marx and Engels argued that human beings are not prisoners of social structures: we make history but we are also the products of history. These insights were disinterred in the social sciences from the 1970s in what became known as 'action' or 'practice' theory: this replaced the domination of either individuals (Box 4.2) or structures with a more nuanced and interdependent relationship between them. The most influential authors on archaeological thought were the British sociologist Anthony Giddens and the French anthropologist Pierre Bourdieu.

GIDDENS, AGENCY AND STRUCTURATION THEORY

Giddens' book, *The Constitution of Society. Outline of a Theory of Structuration* was 'an extended reflection' on Marx's phrase 'Men

---

BOX 4.2 INDIVIDUALS AND INDIVIDUALISM

We use the concept of the individual to highlight difference. As Meskell puts it, 'the individual is a social construction' (1999: 20) (for more on individuals and identities, see Chapter 5). The relationship between us as individuals and members of society is always in flux, with variations in the strength to which we are aware of, and stress, our individuality, our freedom of thought and action. We may argue that we are rational beings who, whether consciously or not, pursue our own aims within society. This is what is called individualism, a Western concept created in the Enlightenment. Within social theory, the primacy of individual action and thought in determining the form of, and changes in, society is called methodological individualism: this is defined as the belief that 'social structures are the unintended consequences of individual actions' (Callinicos 2007: 131) and is an idea contested by both Giddens and Bourdieu. Even in contemporary Western societies, individuals do not exist in splendid isolation; they are also part of complex networks of social, political and economic relationships. This raises a critical question for archaeologists: were these networks more prominent, and individuality less evident, in the precapitalist societies with which we mostly deal?

make history, but not in circumstances of their own choosing' and the 'diversity of complex problems of social analysis this apparently innocuous pronouncement turns out to disclose' (1984: xxi). His central concern was with the relationship between individual actions and the larger-scale structures of which individuals were part. He argued that all social actors/agents are knowledgeable about the social, cultural and natural worlds in which they live, but this knowledgeability is neither unlimited nor guaranteed to produce the desired outcomes (e.g. there may be unintended consequences of our actions). The degree to which individual agents are acting through conscious ('discursive') as opposed to unconscious ('practical') thought, also varies. These actions are pursued and mostly taken for granted (what Giddens calls 'routines') in the context of the everyday lives and 'social practices' of individuals. There is what Giddens called a 'recursive' relationship between social practices and social structure: rather than one determining the other, 'the structural properties of social systems are both the medium and the outcome of the practices that constitute these systems' (1984: 36–7). The social system as a whole is produced and reproduced during the course of this active relationship between practice and structure.

This is the barest outline of Giddens' **theory of structuration**, by which the intertwined relationship between social structure and daily practice by members of a society is central to their socialisation and to the reproduction of, or change in, that structure. In Giddens' text (1984: 9), he argues that **agency** refers to the capability of people (rather than their intentions) to do things in the course of their everyday lives. We will return to definitions of agency, but first let us look at Bourdieu's theory.

BOURDIEU AND HABITUS

If you find Giddens' structuration theory a bit on the heavy side, then at first sight you may be put off by the sometimes inaccessible prose of Bourdieu's (1977) *Outline of a Theory of Practice*. It is worth remembering that he shares with Giddens an interest in the relationships between social practices and structures as they are worked out in everyday lives, and that you will gain a better initial understanding of Bourdieu's concepts and arguments by starting with commentaries on his work. For example, Gosden (1999: 124–6) shows clearly how Bourdieu's famous concept of **'habitus'** was derived from an earlier French anthropologist Marcel Mauss and refers to 'habits which are socially learnt and transmitted'. As well as quoting Bourdieu, Gosden writes as follows:

> Habitus is a second nature. People produce thought, perception and action without thinking about how they are doing so, but in a manner which has its own inherent logic. Social life is neither made up of wild and unpredictable improvisation not the mechanical reproduction of social rules. Habitus is learnt through the process of socialization: through imitation and encouragement rather than through conscious learning.
>
> (1999: 126–7)

The archaeologist Christine Hastorf (2003: 307) cites Bourdieu and writes of how 'people, in their daily lives are routinized, gaining knowledge as well as social skills through experience and observation', and that 'just as practical competence is passed on to children through the enactments of daily chores, activities, stories and justifications, so too are the community values of production and worldview'. She refers to habitus as 'the unspoken way of doing things in a person's daily world' and goes on to write this:

> Each action is only an imperfect citation of the norm, which is created through past practices and remembrances of the way to do things. Within the routines, slippage occurs in the completion of tasks, hence people (as agents) change their tasks over time, through their practices (situations and meanings) of the routines (structures).

These commentaries on Bourdieu's work show its links to that of Giddens, as well as raise important questions. How far do the theories of Giddens and Bourdieu focus overly on social and cultural reproduction rather than change? It is one thing to argue that agents have 'capabilities', but how and when will these powers be exercised? As with all theoretical approaches derived from modern societies, should we impose modern, cross-cultural conceptions of the individual (see below) on to the precapitalist societies of the past? These questions have been taken up by archaeologists trying to make Giddens' and Bourdieu's theories useful for interpreting the past, especially using the concept of agency.

AGENCY IN ARCHAEOLOGY

Postprocessual archaeologists began to cite the works of Giddens and Bourdieu during the early 1980s, with the expansion of case studies during the following decade. But it was not until the early 2000s that we could read either a major review article (Dornan 2002) or an edited book (Dobres and Robb 2000) that discussed the concept of agency and the ways in which it was being applied to archaeology. By this time, Hegmon (2003: 221) noted the ubiquity of agency in North American archaeology. But even though Giddens and Bourdieu had become obligatory citations, this did not mean that they were always the basis for theory building or archaeological analysis, nor was there any agreement on what exactly agency meant. For Dobres and Robb (2000: 1), agency had become 'an ambiguous platitude meaning everything and nothing'. They listed 12 different, but not mutually exclusive uses of the concept (2000: 9), and urged archaeologists to 'make a case not only for why the agency concept is useful, but also why their particular approach is more appropriate than others' (2000: 10). Citation of the gurus was not sufficient in itself.

The scales of agency studies range from the individual to the social system, as well as from the short-term to the long-term. Dornan (2002: 309–14) identified five approaches that are most common in archaeological agency: individual intentionality (Box 4.3), collective agency (e.g. factions in society), humans as rational actors, the unintended consequences of social struggle (Box 4.4), and practical rationality and social struggle. The focus of two approaches on humans as rational actors raises issues. Clark and Blake (1994: 17) constructed a model of the development of institutionalised inequality in lowland Mesoamerica, based on 'self-interested competition among political actors vying for prestige or social esteem'. Interestingly, these 'ambitious actors' were male (why, you might ask?) and called 'aggrandizers'. As well as being 'ambitious', such actors are knowledgeable of the social system and the constraints on it, consciously climbing the social ladder depending on favourable environmental conditions and long-term, unintended consequences (Box 4.4) of their cumulative actions. Clark and Blake argued that new social practices are required before the structural change in society and that these practices have to be maintained for a sufficient length of time so that they become 'habitual'. Such rational actor models are not restricted to agency and practice theory (see optimal foraging theory in Chapter 3). Do they have a universal application for the human species? Are some individuals born more ambitious or competitive, as if this were part of their human nature? Do Western ways of thinking about individuality apply to all cultures, both past and present (see Chapter 5).

BOX 4.3 AGENCY AND INDIVIDUALS

It is one thing to construct theoretical arguments giving an active role to individuals in social change, but how can this be studied through archaeological evidence? An early example was Johnson's (1989) use of architectural and documentary sources to trace and interpret the spatial layout of medieval houses in western Suffolk from the fifteenth to the seventeenth centuries A.D. Johnson argues that such houses were intentionally created by their owners within the technical and social constraints of the time. Sir John Langley, the rector of the hamlet of Hawkedon in the mid-sixteenth century, used the location and layout of his house to 'display and confirm his status' within the local community.

But what if we lack documentary sources? Hodder (2000: 22) proposes the study of 'individual lived lives starting off with the traces of individual events'. Within archaeology, the most direct and frequent combinations of individuals and events are seen in burials. The discovery in 1991 of the body of the late fourth millennium B.C. 'Ice Man' (Otzi) in a glacier in the Otzaler Alps on the border between Austria and Italy caused a sensation. Not only was the body well-preserved, but so also were his hunting equipment and his clothing, enabling archaeologists to build knowledge of his diet, health and activities. His 'lived life' was divided between these isolated harsh uplands and the denser, and more extensive, social networks of lowland, agricultural communities. This was a life, as Hodder (2000: 27) puts it, with 'contradictions between dependency and self-sufficiency'. It was also lived against the background of wider social, economic and ideological changes in Europe and how individuals such as the Ice Man reacted to, and acted on, these changes during the course of their lives.

BOX 4.4 AGENCY AND UNINTENDED CONSEQUENCES

Much ink has been spilt in archaeology on the significance of monuments in human societies. Who built them, why were they built and what did they mean? Were they the outcome of the political, social or ideological strategies of specific individuals? Good examples of such monuments are seen in the pre-Columbian 'Mississippian' plat-form mounds in the south-eastern United States (e.g. at Cahokia, on the eastern edge of the modern city of St. Louis), built as focal points within their own settlements and centralised regional-scale political and social hierarchies. But was the construction of these mounds and the emergence of polities really the intended outcome of ambitious, scheming members of elite groups? Pauketat (2000) proposes a dif-ferent interpretation. The central archaeological observation is that the platform mounds were built in stages, rather than as a single, pur-posive construction. 'At and around Cahokia, there are often nearly as many individual stages...within mounds as there were years within which the mounds were built', with the impressively large Monks Mound (291 m × 236 m and 30 m high) showing 'incremental enlarge-ments and a regular construction cycle' (Pauketat 2000: 119). Mound construction was not just important in itself but partly 'an effort that brought people together on a regular basis' (2000: 120). Rather than leaders constructing mounds and centres exploiting people's labour and according to established blueprints, the regular assembly of the mound builders contributed not only to the construction and sym-bolism of the mounds but also to the emergence itself of a more hierarchical and centralised society. This emergence was not, as usu-ally portrayed, the result of conscious, coercive design by elites with a cunning plan, but as much (if not more) the unintended outcome of existing, traditional ritual practices. 'Once constrained by the spaces and practices of the new Mississippian formations, the coordinated political actions necessary to objectively "resist" domination – with or without elite actions – would have been inhibited' (2000: 123).

Archaeological studies of agency are not exclusively based on prac-tice theory and may involve the construction of intellectual bridges with other theories. Authors who may be labelled 'processualist', 'postprocessualist', 'Marxist', 'neo-Darwinist', etc., integrate agency in their interpretations of the past. McGuire (2002: 144) argued that 'we should seek our explanations for history in the real dialectical interplay of nature, structure, culture and agency in the specific cases we study' at the level of the group rather than the individual, given Marx's affirmation that 'humans make history as social beings'. Shennan (1993) has argued that similar issues arise in both practice theory and evolutionary analyses of social behaviour, but that Darwinian approaches give an account of cultural transmission that is lacking in Giddens' structuration theory. The two approaches are seen as complementary. Whatever the theoretical make-up of agency studies in archaeology, it is not an issue of the wholesale borrowing of concepts and theories: as Dobres and Robb (2000: 14) put it 'we need to address how contemporary agency theory should be modified to fit archaeological research interests, archaeological scales of inquiry, and the unique qualities of archaeological data'.

'Agents' or 'actors' also crop up in two other bodies of theory, **actor network theory** (which raises the question as to whether objects, as well as people, have agency, see Chapter 5) and **agent-based modelling** (which has grown in popularity during the last two decades and is a form of computer-based modelling). At the basis of this modelling is the interaction of individual and collective (e.g. households, villages) agents with their (social and natural) environments and how this leads, or might lead, to the emergence of new 'properties' of social systems (e.g. hereditary inequality, hierarchical settlement systems, urbanism). Although such computer simulations are highly simplified, they have become useful and stimulating tools for developing our understanding of theoretical arguments (e.g. how population dynamics relate to social or subsistence change) and how they relate to the 'real world' data we see in the archaeological record (e.g. Kohler 2012).

MEMORY AND BIOGRAPHY

SOCIAL MEMORY

If human agency works through social practices, then it draws on experience and memory. But what is this 'memory', what does it do, how is it acted out and transmitted from generation to generation?

A good starting point is to stress the difference between personal memories (e.g. where you were on 9/11) and social or collective memories (e.g. memorials to soldiers who died in two world wars) which are created, shared and transmitted through generations by social groups. The concept of memory, as something social as opposed to personal, has been discussed recently by historians, anthropologists and philosophers (e.g. Connerton 1989; Rowlands 1993). All recognise that **social memory** is used to refer to 'the selective preservation, construction, and obliteration of ideas about the way things were in the past, in service of some interest in the present' (Van Dyke 2011: 237).

Two writers have been particularly influential in the use of social memory in archaeological theory. Paul Connerton (1989) made a distinction between two forms of memory practices: inscribed memory (involving monuments, written texts and representations of various kinds) and embodied memory (that is bodily rituals and behaviour, including performance). Michael Rowlands (1993) made a comparable division between inscribing practices (focusing on frequently repeated rituals, publicly visible in acts like the construction and use of monuments) and incorporating practices (what Connerton called embodied memory), with more secret and exclusive practices that leave less visible archaeological traces. As with all such typologies, they are open to the criticism that they are somewhat simplistic (e.g. Van Dyke 2011: 236), but they have focused attention on the ways and media through which memory of social institutions and identities is constructed, expressed, performed and transmitted. Van Dyke and Alcock (2003: 4–5) define four overlapping kinds of material media through which social memory works: ritual behaviour (e.g. monuments, cults, acts of votive deposition), narratives (expressed through writing, oral traditions), objects and representations on them (e.g. figurines, art) and specific places 'inscribed with meaning' (e.g. places/sites in landscapes). Their material nature opens the way for study in archaeological contexts. Given the extensive literature, let us look only at examples of social memory enacted through ritual practices, places and objects.

RITUAL PRACTICES

Ritual practices are not restricted to belief systems and religions, but also occur in secular contexts. The formality, repetitiveness and prescribed performances that characterise rituals are present in a variety of contexts from the Catholic Mass (sacred) to the university lecture (secular). In the social sciences as a whole, prescribed ritual performances have been extensively studied in rites of passage (e.g. birth, marriage and death) and feasting. Death ruptures the social order, leaving gaps (e.g. in families, identity groups, public offices) and requiring them to be filled. The performance of death rituals varies in form, scale and inclusiveness (comparatively few of us have state funerals or memorial services) while symbolism may vary between cultures (burials under the floors of Early Bronze Age houses in south-east Spain do not symbolise the acts of serial killers, as would be the case of in our own society). All death rituals draw upon established practice, that is upon social memory, and by the ways in which these rituals are enacted they may construct and legitimate new memories.

Hamilakis (1998) presents a well-documented study of the consumption of food and drink in feasting associated with mortuary practices in the Aegean Bronze Age, suggesting that social memories (for example, of specific individuals) were intended both to remember and forget or erase. Other examples of such 'forgetting' as part of social memory in past ritual practices range widely from the Mesolithic of south-east Europe (Boric 2010) to Early Medieval Europe (Williams 2003).

PLACES

The social rituals and practices we study as archaeologists occurred in places at a variety of scales, from individual lifetimes to millennia and from the individual house to landscapes. Funerary monuments have life histories and what are called 'biographies' (see below), with cycles of construction, use, rebuilding, abandonment and even re-use up to several millennia later. In Western Europe, there are many examples of these practices in Neolithic monuments (Diaz-Guardamino *et al.* 2015): megalithic tombs (as well as prehistoric rock art sites) were appropriated by being Christianised symbolically and even by superimposition of chapels on top of tomb mounds, while other tombs were reused for burials and deposition of objects, linking them to mythical ancestors. In Greece, half a millennium after their construction and use, Mycenaean tombs received offerings of pottery and votive objects and were used for sacrifices as part of strategies to appropriate the past to legitimate the present (Alcock 1991). New social memories were being created, not only within and on tombs but also in the landscapes in which they stood.

Life histories are also seen in houses and settlements, the immediate surroundings in which people live and, following Bourdieu and Giddens, act out their daily social practices, drawing on the past for the knowledge and bodily skills necessary for the construction of their built environment. There may be variations in the life-cycles of individual houses and their location within settlement areas, as memories of past inhabitants are incorporated in house biographies. Hodder (2019) uses the concept of 'history houses' to argue for the importance of social memory in the reproduction of social life at Neolithic Catalhoyuk. For the Roman Empire, Boozer (2010: 138) argues that 'individuals and groups invoke memories of the past to denote their social identity and their placement within the empire'. Furthermore, 'mastery of Roman culture, regardless of one's origin, was an important component of patronage and privilege' and that 'knowledge of mythology became an effective status marker that unified the elite across the Roman Empire' (2010: 151). In the case of house 1 in the Roman town of Amheida in southwest Egypt, the wall paintings included representations of Homeric, Greek and Roman mythologies, showing 'a deep mythological past' (lasting some 1,500 years) and declaring that 'the occupant possessed the education and creativity associated with elite members of the Roman Empire' (2010: 152). This was in contrast to a second house that lacked the Homeric representations and showed no preference for Roman of Egyptian identity.

OBJECTS

Different rituals, held at different kinds of places, are materialised through objects. Forms, uses and symbolism may change during the lifetimes of objects, which have histories (e.g. they may be exchanged or appropriated by new owners) and embody memories. Steel (2013: 191) traces the life history of a Bronze Age object from Cyprus from its use as rubber for grinding grain, subsequently reworked as a gaming stone, then walled into a building foundation and lastly to its current display as a museum artefact. As Steel writes,

> its cultural significance, along with the way it was used and viewed by the people who created, modified and encountered it, would have changed as it was transformed into a distinct new object with very different uses and social connotations.

Such a life history, or **biography** (Gosden and Marshall 1999), may see objects transferred between different owners, used in social relations and acquiring different values for themselves and, by association, their owners. Heirlooms of all kinds act as memory aids, reminding us of our links to ancestral pasts that may span decades and centuries. Such heirlooms may have a social value that far transcends their functional one (Box 4.5).

BOX 4.5 SECONDARY BURIAL AND RITUAL HEIRLOOMS

Kuijt (2008) studies ritual heirlooms within the context of the treatment of the dead in the Near Eastern Neolithic. The period of the eleventh to tenth millennia BC marked a change in subsistence practices in the Near East, alongside social change and population aggregation in large villages (known as the Middle Pre-Pottery Neolithic B period). What used to seem like a rather idiosyncratic, local practice of plastering and painting disinterred skulls is now interpreted as a sequence of primary and secondary burial. Kuijt (2008) documents the ritual practices after death, from small-scale primary burial over a short period of time, through the later removal of skulls from the burials, the painting and plastering of these skulls and the larger-scale use of the skulls in further public ritual practices to their reburial, individually and in groups in houses and courtyards (Figure 4.1). Kuijt's study is detailed and ties in these ritual practices to both the construction of collective memory (e.g. note the painted and plastered skulls are not direct representations of the dead individuals, but what he calls idealised representations, that is a change from a known individual to a collective memory) and the forgetting of certain individuals later in time.

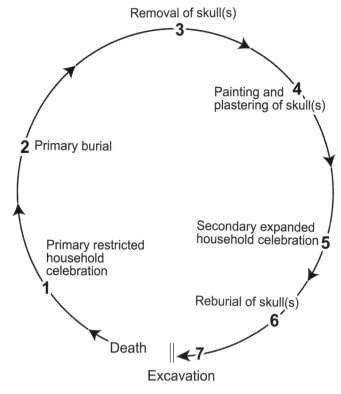

Figure 4.1 Successive ritual practices (1–6) from death to skull reburial in the Near East Middle Pre-Pottery Neolithic B period. A more schematic version of Kuijt (2008: Figure 2) with the addition of a stage of excavation. Each stage from 1 to 6 takes place over a variable length of time. The length of time between stage 6 and excavation in stage 7 takes place over 12 millennia.

TIME AND SPACE

The use of the concept of memory in the social sciences has both strengths and weaknesses (see Van Dyke 2011: 240–5). However, we define social memory and through whatever material media it works, it enables us and enabled our ancestors to view, understand and create their and our pasts. We live with these pasts all around us. Our material world is made up of multiple pasts (e.g. buildings of different dates, materials such as heirlooms inherited from one generation after another) situated all around us in different places and at different scales. Although time and space are fundamental dimensions with which we build chronological sequences and material culture groupings, they are more than backdrops to human activities. We define periods and areas in time and space as a means to trace what we regard as relevant changes in the past (e.g. in political units and organisations), but both of these dimensions were also lived in and experienced by human communities at different scales. As we have seen with ideas on human agency and social memory, time and space play important roles in cultural transmission, they shape what we do as social beings and, in turn, we shape them (Hadji and Souvatzi 2014). Memory is embedded culturally in time and space beyond our individual lifetimes, as seen in the genealogies of social groups. As such, time and space are important constructs in archaeological theory and in the construction of histories.

SOCIAL IDENTITIES

The discussion of culture in this chapter presents ideas on the meaning and symbolism of our material world, as well as the ways in which social beings (whether individuals or groups) play active roles in the construction and understanding of that world and its histories. A key concept in this theory building is that of **social identity**, the study of which has grown in frequency and importance since the early 1990s (Meskell 2002: fig 1; Pierce, et al. 2016, Fig 1.1).

WHAT IS IDENTITY?

Diaz–Andreu and Lucy (2005: 1) define identity as an 'individual's identification with broader groups on the basis of differences socially sanctioned as significant'. These 'broader groups' include ethnicity, nationality, class, age, gender, sexuality, political affiliation, social status, religion, disability and so on, helping us to 'define who we are, who we are not, what we can do, where we can go, how we dress, and a myriad, other things' (2005: 11). Such identities are both socially and culturally constructed, and individuals clearly have a combination of identities: you may identify yourself as a white, middle-class, transsexual female, or a working-class, heterosexual male of colour or one of a range of other combinations of identities. Such identities are what Johnson (2020: 172) calls 'variable, unstable, complex, fluid and changing, rather than being simple, fixed, or essential or only a matter of biology'. According to circumstances and individual agency, there are complex interactions between your different individual identities (what is called **intersectionality**, a concept introduced into archaeology under the influence of third-wave feminism, see below). The relative importance that may be placed on these identities (e.g. on your class relations as opposed to your ethnicity) also varies. Overall, the nature of, and change in, your individual identity is argued to play an important role in what you can and cannot do at different stages of your lifetime and in different contexts. Meskell (2002) provides detailed discussion and extensive examples of how the influence of Marxist, Feminist and other theoretical approaches has shaped the study of identity and its relation to politics.

ETHNICITY

In the first half of the twentieth century, archaeologists aimed to define 'peoples' by consistent clusters of material culture within marked boundaries through periods of time. The flaws and complexities in how 'peoples' were materially expressed were exposed in Hodder (1978). During the 1990s, archaeologists turned their attention to ethnic groups rather than 'peoples', and to ethnicity as a social identity. Jones (1997: xii) defined it as 'that aspect of a person's self-conceptualization which results from identification with a broader group in opposition to others on the basis of perceived cultural differentiation and/or common descent'. Ethnic groups were self-defining and ethnicity was constructed and maintained through socialisation and social memory. An important contemporary example of self-identification can be seen in the ability of Northern Ireland citizens to identify as either British or Irish, as part of the peace process in the Good Friday Agreement of 1999. The past has been appropriated in the present in the construction of nationality and nationalism, as seen in the case of Nazi Germany, or denied (in spite of the archaeological evidence to the contrary) in Rhodesia (now Zimbabwe) under illegal white rule in the 1960s and 1970s.

FEMINISM AND GENDER

The theoretical roots of gender studies lie in **feminism**, defined by Gilchrist (1999: xiv) as 'the political conviction to challenge existing power relations between men and women'. These power relations range from women's control of their own bodies (e.g. abortion rights) to equal rights to education and employment (e.g. breaking 'glass ceilings'). Not only does this involve political activism (such as securing the right to vote), but also challenges to widespread, deep-rooted assumptions of women's roles in production, the division of labour and how women are portrayed in everyday life. Underlying these assumptions was the belief that there were 'natural' (i.e. biological) inequalities between the sexes, although this was influentially challenged by Engels (1972).

The development of feminism in the social sciences and more widely in Western society has been divided into three 'waves' (Table 4.2), although there are differences in their definition (see Gilchrist 1999: 2–3; Meskell 1999: 54–6). Fourth, fifth and sixth waves have emerged in the last decade, but have not made the same impacts on archaeology. The agendas of the first wave (e.g. women's suffrage rights) were expanded in late 1960s' second-wave challenges to the patriarchy, that is, the 'power relations that structure the subordination of women, through institutions such as the family, education, religion and government' (Gilchrist 1999: 2). This wave was also influenced by Marxist feminists in social sciences such as anthropology (e.g. Leacock 1983). The themes of the third wave were heavily influenced by different strands of postmodernism. From the second to the third waves, **gender** became a central concept of feminism and was viewed as 'socially produced and historically changing' (Gilchrist 1999: 2). Gender was a matter of culture, distinct from the biology of sex, although this difference became more nuanced in the third wave (see below). If gender was socially and culturally constructed, then there could be more than a male and a female gender, expressed through culture and material culture. Examples of third-genders are readily seen in the present day and in the historical past (see Gilchrist 1999: 58–64). This emphasis on culture, as opposed to biology, also led to conflict with Darwinian approaches to human behaviour and reproductive strategies (Gilchrist 1999: 10–13).

Archaeology was slow off the mark in its adoption of feminism and the study of gender. Conkey and Spector (1984) were the first to launch a sustained critique of male-centred bias (**androcentrism**) and gender power relations in archaeology. This was seen in the ways in which stereotypes of men and women shaped their participation in archaeology, from everyday division of labour in fieldwork, through definition and pursuit of research subjects (e.g. field or laboratory based), to relative access to funding for this research, and the lack of prominent roles for women in the discipline. Modern, Western views of male and female roles in everyday life and society were projected into the past. Men were hunters, women were gatherers. Men were metallurgists, women were potters. Ethnographic analogies showed that the division of labour was much more complex than these stereotypical assumptions (see also Gilchrist 1999: 32–6).

In addition to this critique of androcentrism, Conkey and Spector (1984: 23–36) used the example of feminist approaches to anthropology as a guide to the ways in which we might construct an archaeology of gender. They wondered why an archaeological study of gender should be any more challenging, given the nature of the available data, than the other social and cultural themes studied by both processual and postprocessual archaeologists. Like these other themes, they argued for the need of both theory building and the

Table 4.2 Three waves of feminism

First wave:	women's rights to suffrage, education, employment, late nineteenth/early twentieth centuries
Second wave:	women's liberation movement, contraception, legalised abortion from late 1960s, challenges to the patriarchy
Third wave:	gender as socially and culturally constructed, more than two genders, difference = no single female 'character'/experience, range of identities from 1980s

development of methods that will enable archaeologists to pursue the study of gender.

These criticisms and challenges for gender archaeology were taken a major step further by the authors in Gero and Conkey (1991). Criticism of androcentrism was taken as a first step, followed by 'remedial research' (Wylie 1991: 32) that introduced women as subjects in society and culture, thereby suggesting alternative pasts in which gender played a part. The third stage was to ask how appropriate and useful archaeological methodologies might be developed for studying gender issues in the past. This does not reduce a feminist archaeology to the simple 'finding' of women in the past, but gender relations are present both in everyday life (and therefore available for study in the archaeological record) and in our own everyday experience of 'doing archaeology'. Gero (1991) reviewed ethnographic examples of women engaging in stone tool production, arguing that differences in biological strength between males and females may be important only at different stages of production (rather than ruling out female participation). Wright (1991) showed that pottery production is undertaken by both men and women. Brumfiel (1991) argued that women's weaving increased in scale in relation to the goods produced as tribute by peoples conquered by the Aztecs.

Since the early 1990s, there has been a major intensification of gender studies in archaeology. An excellent source of case studies on gender, labour and production is provided by Gilchrist (1999: 36–52), who points out that this focus on the division of labour has mainly centred on North America (although it is also seen in Mediterranean Europe). In contrast, gender archaeology in Europe has been more focused on symbolism and culture, especially questions of identity and sexuality.

SEXUALITY

Are humans strictly and exclusively divided into biological males and females, that is two sexes? The human body does not support this claim, as can be seen by variation in combinations of chromosomes and types of reproductive organs (Meskell 1999: 72–4); there is no simple binary division between male and female, nor between masculinity and femininity. What is more, 'categories of biological sex...must also be seen as historically created and contextually perceived' (Gilchrist 1999: 56). For example, the modern, binary distinctions between homo- and hetero-sexuality were the products of late nineteenth-century thought and discussion (see below).

Where does this leave masculinity and femininity? This is an important question for archaeology, as differences in the types and frequencies of artefacts (in human burials, houses and settlements) have often been seen as indicators of distinctive male and female roles and statuses. In the absence or paucity of osteological analysis, the identification of male as opposed to female burials may be made on the basis of assumptions of male/female grave goods. Just as there are stereotypes of what men and women do, so there are the qualities it takes to be masculine and feminine: as Gilchrist (1999: 64) writes, it is assumed that 'men are active, ardent, dominant, aggressive or violent; in contrast to an essential female who is passive, maternal, gentle and tender'. These inherent qualities have been argued to produce male hunters and warriors as opposed to female gatherers and hearth-minders. Treherne (1995) portrayed masculinity in European Bronze Age burials by the presence of artefacts such as weapons, vehicles, horses, drinking vessels and items used for bodily decoration. This interpretation is long, detailed and merits scrutiny, both for its handling of the data and the assumptions of male and female qualities (see the criticisms of Gilchrist 1999: 66–8). Meskell (1999: 61) also uses other case studies to argue that 'there is not one, monolithic masculinity, and we must recognise the interplay of race, class and sexuality' in the construction of 'masculinities'.

Following this argument, differences in sexuality are self-identified and constructed, rather than a once and for all times distinction between what is categorised as natural (heterosexuality) as opposed to abnormal and deviant (homosexuality). A critical contribution to this argument, influenced by the French postmodernist Michel Foucault, was by the American gender theorist Judith Butler, who dismissed the idea of two biological sexes as **heteronormativity**, which ignores a range of historically and culturally specific sexual identities (e.g. as in today's LGBTQ+ communities). Butler (1990) argued that both gender and sexual identities were created by what she called **performance**, or a 'stylized repetition of acts' (1990: 140): Gilchrist (1999: 82) expresses this clearly as 'the repetition of postures, gestures, dress, language and so on, performed as the repeated citation of a gendered norm' and alludes to the debt this concept owes to Bourdieu's habitus. Such learning through culture begins with childhood.

Butler's ideas have been widely, although sometimes uncritically, drawn on in archaeology (see Meskell 1999: 38), and they make an important challenge to wider, often unconscious attempts to project back into the past what are modern, Western ideas and institutions. Her ideas were a contribution to what is called **queer theory**, which developed in the social sciences from the early 1990s and filtered through into archaeology by the end of that decade. At first glance, you might think that this is a theory that is focused on the study and histories of homosexuality. Close examination shows that it is not a theory (hence the often-used reference to 'queer' or 'queering'), nor is it just 'digging for homosexuals' or a 'manifesto for promoting homosexuals' (Dowson 2000: 165). Definitions by archaeologists vary. Johnson (2020: 292) calls it 'an approach that rejects traditional categories of gender and sexuality' which 'seeks to destabilize these categories, and frequently focuses on sexual and gender ambiguities and mismatches'. Croucher (2005: 611) argues for much broader and more inclusive definition, part of

> a package of approaches which challenge the unjustified projection of modern values and beliefs onto the past, exploring alternative ways of being in and experiencing the world, including sexuality, gender, identity, personhood, families, human/animal relationships, labour and ideologies in the past.

Such variation raises an important question: does it impede or support research on case studies? You may already be wondering how useful specifically archaeological case studies of sexuality identities might be, given the evidence available to us? Schmidt and Voss (2000) presented the first collection of papers on sexuality research in archaeology, followed by Voss's (2008) review of the kinds of themes being studied by archaeologists from both prehistoric and historic contexts.

LOOKING FORWARD

The theories presented in this chapter were the focus of attention in postprocessual archaeology. By the 1990s, some theories had been found wanting, while this decade also saw the growth of agency publications, along with more detailed studies of cultural transmission and social identities. Very different theories and theoretical gurus were beginning to be cited by archaeologists in the 1990s. These marked substantial changes in the ways in which we view and study our material world, as you will see in Chapter 5.

SUMMARY

- The material objects studied by archaeologists do not serve solely functional purposes. They also have meanings, they symbolise something about our cultural worlds and our identities as social beings. But what is 'culture' as opposed to 'material culture'? What role(s) does culture play in shaping human action and social change? What kinds of 'identities' do we have?

- The context of these debates was situated in a major change in the intellectual landscape of the social sciences since the late 1960s. Modernism was challenged by postmodernism as a way of studying and understanding ourselves, our cultures and our societies. Postmodernists rejected major bodies of thought such as Marxism, but also came under attack for their relativism and their inadequate grasp of how science works.

- Like Marxism, postmodernists recognised that our social, political and cultural standpoints impact on our understandings of the present and the past.

- The concept of culture has a variety of definitions, but in the social sciences it is argued that it is socially transmitted. Material culture is both a material product and a part of culture. Its symbolism and meanings were central to postprocessual archaeology. Structuralism was drawn from anthropology to identify unconscious rules, structures and beliefs in culture; in other words, culture was like a language. In contrast, poststructuralists argued that culture was read as a text.

- Archaeologists also drew upon theoretical arguments in anthropology and sociology in the 1980s to study the relationship between social structures and individual, human agency. Both Giddens' theory of structuration and Boudieu's concept of habitus proposed a nuanced view of this relationship, situating it within the context of everyday lives and individual social practices (hence 'practice theory'). Archaeologists used different definitions of 'agency' and different approaches to its study during the 1980s and 1990s. They also drew on the concepts of social memory and biography in cultural transmission between the generations.

- The concept of social identity became increasingly popular in archaeology during the 1990s and early twenty-first century. Identities include those of ethnicity, class, gender and sexuality. Such identities are socially and culturally constructed and are materially expressed in various ways. Archaeological studies of gender since the 1980s drew on feminism and its successive 'waves', while sexuality in past societies only became a focus for research from the late 1990s.

FURTHER READING

Good introductions to the range of social theories covered in this chapter can be found in Callinicos (2007) and Inglis and Thorpe (2019). Butler (2002) gives a short and accessible coverage of post-modernism, while Knapp (1996) critically reviews its influence on archaeology. Issues and examples of archaeological research by, and for indigenous communities, including the challenges of multivo-cality, are covered informatively by Atalay (2008) and Bruchac *et al.* (2010). The handbook edited by Tilley *et al.* (2006) includes studies of structuralist, semiotic, poststructuralist, agency and biographical approaches to material culture. Lechte (1994: 35–86) gives short introductions to a range of structuralist authors, while Hodder and Hutson (2003: 45–74) present examples of structuralist and poststructuralist archaeologies. Belsey (2002) is an introduction to poststructuralism. Issues of structure, agency and social reproduction in archaeology are reviewed in detail by Dobres and Robb (2000). A comparable volume on social memory, covering both theoretical issues and archaeological applications, was edited by Van Dyke and Alcock (2003), while Connerton's (1989) book is still a good source on the theory of how societies remember. Diaz-Andreu *et al.* (2005) provide an overview of the archaeology of identity. The best intro-duction to feminism and gender remains that of Gilchrist (1999), while a range of case studies on gender and sexuality are presented in Gero and Conkey (1991), Hays-Gilpin and Whitley (1998) and Schmidt and Voss (2000).

BEING IN A MATERIAL WORLD

The past was different. We think as modern, Western, human beings, brought up within our world of cultural beliefs and practices. We have used concepts from 'our' world, such as technology, economy and society, to think about 'other' worlds. As the anthropologist Tim Ingold (2000: 314) points out, 'economic relations are embedded in social relations' (see Chapter 2). We may refer to prehistoric structures as 'houses' or sites as 'towns', or draw upon contemporary, ethnographic analogies to describe societies as 'chiefdoms', and there is an argument that such categorisation can be productive starting points for thinking about the past. But working from the present to the past in our modernist, Western ways can also be misleading: do these concepts enable or constrain our research? In the last two decades, archaeologists have embraced a range of new theoretical approaches, both 'new' and 'post', and tried to think in radically different ways about the past as 'other' worlds. These approaches have been adopted in our discipline under the title of 'relational archaeologies'. Together, they challenge many of the bases of Chapters 2–4. They are the subject of this chapter.

BEGINNING TO THINK IN DIFFERENT WAYS

A WORLD OF DUALISMS?

An important criticism of modernist ways of thinking (raised within postmodernist thought) is the way we divide how we perceive ourselves and the world around us in terms of polarised **dualisms** (also known as 'Cartesian dualisms' after the seventeenth-century

DOI: 10.4324/9781315657097-5

French philosopher René Descartes).You will have come across such dualisms (including those of structuralist theory) in Chapters 1–4: for example, culture/nature, simple/complex societies, mind/matter (or body), domestic/ritual (or profane/sacred), and agency/structure. But how far do such dualisms help us to think about the worlds of present and past peoples? Is not reality more complex than this? Dividing the essence of human beings into opposing categories of 'mind' and 'matter' is, at the very least, blurred by the argument that 'mind' is matter that thinks.And remember the discussion in Chapter 4 of differences between 'males' and 'females' and the complexity of gender and sex identities. Mind/matter and male /female dualisms are part of a broader opposition of culture and nature, or human and animal.

The sharpness of these distinctions has initially become blurred by the existence of multiple definitions of both culture (see Chapter 4) and nature. The discipline of anthropology has a history of debates on the meaning of culture and has now reached the point at which use of the concept is increasingly questioned. Even those who still find value in talking about different cultures recognise that these are not clear, bounded entities. Many indigenous societies have different concepts of culture and nature to our own. Their different ways of thinking about the world have led anthropologists to argue that 'nature is a construct of culture' (Metcalf 2005: 115). A famous example of this difference can be seen in the belief of the indigenous Ojibwa people of Central Canada that stones are alive, animate rather than inanimate, moving and making sounds (Ingold 2018: 17–25) – an initially strange idea that challenges our view that agency is a distinctively human quality.

What of the usual claim that a characteristic of human beings, as opposed to animals, is that we make things, whether we call them artefacts or objects?We conceive of artefacts that we hope and intend will be solutions to our needs (e.g. better tools for working timber used in house construction) and then pursue our designs using the raw materials of 'nature'.We are the subject and nature is the object. We, as opposed to animals, have both culture and material culture. But studies of animals who use and make things show that this is not an exclusive human characteristic (Humle 2010). For example, birds make nests, beavers make lodges and dams and chimpanzees hunt termites by poking sharpened sticks into their mounds. Ingold (2000: 65–7) shows how the construction of nests by male weaverbirds is not a matter of instinct as opposed to culture. Although the bird does not have 'the specification of an innate, genetically transmitted design' and unlike humans 'almost certainly' does not have a mental picture of 'the final form of construction', it has to use its bodily capacities and skills learned 'through practice and experience in an environment' (as do humans). The difference(s) between humans and animals is more nuanced, with the humans developing social transmission of culture, larger-scale and more complex networks of social relations, and new needs, beliefs and aims in life.

MATERIALITY: JUST ANOTHER BUZZWORD?

Clearly there are problems with seeing the past through the modern lens of such dualisms as culture/nature and human/animal (Harris and Cipolla 2017: 27–32). A key concept in helping us to move forward, and one which was a buzzword in archaeology in the early part of this millennium, is **materiality**. As with the concept of agency, there are problems with its definition. Knappett (2012: 188) refers to its 'varied and often inconsistent usage' in archaeology 'as if mere mention of materiality is sometimes seen as enough' (201). Ingold (2007: 2) recalls attending an anthropology conference on materiality at which no speaker 'was able to say what materiality actually means'!

Let us look at three examples of how archaeologists define what materiality is (Table 5.1) Central to these definitions are closely intertwined material (between human beings and the worlds in which they live) and social relationships (the roles and importance of materials in the social lives of human beings). Artefacts are socially and culturally constructed (e.g. in their design and their symbolism), while the materials of which they are made have physical and mechanical properties

Table 5.1 Three definitions of materiality

1. Graves Brown (2001: 1): 'how the very material character of the world around us is appropriated by humanity'.
2. Boivin (2008: 25–6): while 'material' includes 'all that is tangible rather than abstract' in the world (e.g. objects, landscapes, human bodies) and 'material culture' refers to the things and objects made by people, materiality stresses 'the physicality of the material world' and how it enables and constrains action by this physicality.
3. Pollard (2004: 48): 'how the material character of the world is comprehended, appropriated and involved in human projects'

that are important for the functional and stylistic characteristics of the resulting artefacts and more generally for social life. 'Aspects of cultural choice determine both the material composition and the mechanical properties of material culture' (Jones 2002: 66). The making of artefacts is more than the simple following of mental templates' (what Ingold (2013: 31) calls 'the imposition of preconceived forms on raw material substance'), but a more complex process in which the artefact producer brings together bodily skills (e.g. strength, balance) with the properties of materials in a process of what Jones (2012) calls 'practical performance'. The builders of many Gothic cathedrals did not work with architectural plans and these impressive monuments should be understood as 'sites of experimental practice, as places at which people, practices and diverse, but amorphous, materials can be shaped, manipulated and assembled' (2012: 16–17). There was room for creativity in the relationship between builders and materials. Such 'performance' can be seen in all kinds of material culture categories (Box 5.1).

BOX 5.1 MAKERS AND MATERIALS

Making is not a mechanical process. Whatever the artefact type, its production is not a simple matter of replication. As Jones (2012: 105–19) shows with regard to pottery production in Neolithic Orkney that, if replication were the central factor, then this would not account for observed rates of continuity and change. In the case of Neolithic rock art in Argyll (Scotland), the raw material (i.e. the rock itself) was carefully selected, not only in terms of its location in the landscape, but also for geologically created cracks and fissures in its surfaces. Jones (2012: 77–85) shows how there was a relationship between specific motifs and specific forms of these cracks and fissures. The motifs were not imposed on the rock, but 'worked into the pre-existing geological features of the rock'. Colour contrasts are revealed between the rock and the luminescent quartz used to produce the art, while weathering of the rock may reduce the visibility of the art. The light at different times of the day also affects visibility of the art: most of the motifs were deliberately carved on rock outcrops facing the early morning and evening sunlight. As Jones puts it, 'rock art carvers enhanced shadows and manipulated light' (84), 'performing' the hiding and revelation of the art.

The focus on the symbolism and meaning of artefacts in the archaeology of the 1970s to the 1990s often did not recognise and study this intertwining of the material and social worlds. Following on from the example of Gosden's (1994) discussion of materiality, Jones (2004: 328) argued that 'the linguistic or textual metaphor has its limitations, as it treats the material world as a mere substratum on which humans lay their ideas and concepts' and 'the material qualities of objects and the way in which they impinged on human beings was not fully acknowledged'. The use and meaning of material culture could not be studied without attention to its material qualities. This critique of structuralist and poststructuralist approaches to the study of material culture was continued in Boivin's (2008: 46–7) argument that, rather than 'ideas and cultural understandings' existing in people's minds and then 'materialised by attaching them to appropriate symbols', there are many cases in which they 'do not precede, but rather are helped into becoming by the material world and human engagement with it'. Rather than this 'engagement' being the imposition of a separate 'mind' over 'matter', both 'continually bring each other into being' (2008: 23) (see also Renfrew 2012).

WHERE DO WE GO FROM HERE?

Consider two questions that arise from this discussion and may help us to think in different ways about the past:

1 Should we now completely discard thinking in modernist dualisms about the past?
2 If non-humans have some form of agency, do we need to change our archaeological ontology from one which pursues representations of the past (e.g. histories, processes or meanings) to one which studies the interdependent relationships between humans, non-humans and materials? Is being (or living) in the material world not about human subjects acting on a passive, exterior material world, but the outcomes of complex inter-relationships involving equally important actors, whether human or not?

Given that you have now read the case for discarding dualisms, the rest of this chapter will concentrate on question 2. Let us start with the human engagement with the material world. How do we engage with, or experience, the material world in which we live? Yes, we use material culture but, more importantly, we act through the senses of the human body.

EXPERIENCING THE WORLD

THE BODY IN THEORY

We have already seen how Marx argued that the body was important as an instrument of labour in the production of the basic requirements for human life. Artefacts were also extensions of the body. Darwinian theories would be unthinkable without the human body. Chris Shilling (2012: 25–44) notes the rare attention given to the body by thinkers such as Marx, Weber and Durkheim. In the 1960s and 1970s, both structuralism and poststructuralism focussed on the study of consciousness and language, but the body as a whole 'was portrayed as a passive shell activated by the creative minds of individuals' (2012: 30). It was only in the 1980s and 1990s that 'body studies' took off in social theory, in the wider context of political, economic and cultural changes in the Western world.

Shilling presents two ways of thinking about the human body. Naturalistic approaches 'conceptualise the body as a pre-social, biological basis on which rests the superstructure of self-identity and society: the capacities and constraints of human bodies define individuals, generating the socio-economic relations that characterise national and international patterns of living' (Shilling 2012: 45). Think of the discredited claims made for the female capacities for action, judgment and employment being limited by their hormones. Such claims were seized on and amplified by what was called **sociobiology**, which drew on Darwinian and neo-Darwinian theory to attribute such inequalities between males and females, or between people of different races or ethnicities, to differences in their brains, their genes or their physical make-up in general. The social was reduced to the biological. The alternative way of thinking was that the body was socially constructed. In this case, opinion was divided between how far the social influenced, or even determined, the biological. For both social scientists and archaeologists, the most influential constructivist voice was that of Michel Foucault, who focussed almost entirely on the body as socially constructed, how power was exercised on and through the body, its movements and daily actions, in a variety of public institutions (e.g. schools, prisons, asylums), downplaying the specific historical contexts in which this construction took place, and side-stepping any conception of the body as 'an active, material component of social action' (Shilling 2012: 84).

Is there a more convincing position on the human body, rather than it being conceived of as either biologically or socially constructed? Shilling's answer to this question is clear and concise: 'the body is a social and biological entity shaped by, while also forming a basis for, society' (2012: 107). Our bodies change during our lifetimes in relation to complex relations between our age, gender, diet, employment and social grouping. Bodily change is also the result of social and cultural choices. Think of the ways in which people seek to express their social identity through tattoos and resist the appearance of ageing through cosmetic surgery and strenuous exercise. Think about transplant surgery, pacemakers and so on, that make the body cultural as well as biological. Ideas about diet, ideal body image including appearance and weight (e.g. in relation to concepts of what looks masculine or feminine) are shaped by culture. The body here is manipulated to fit expectations set by the media and advertising, let alone the careers of ridiculous celebrities! This is the body as an object and a commodity, shaped by society and culture. Even the ways in which we talk and walk are shaped by our upbringing and education. Overall, as Robb and Harris (2013: 16) argue, 'there is no opposition between an underlying biological body and a veneer of a social body'. These are all valuable insights, but they would be incomplete without the introduction of a major body of theory drawn from continental European philosophy.

PHENOMENOLOGY AND THE SENSES

Let us begin with a definition. The sociologists David Inglis and Christopher Thorpe (2019: 78) write that 'phenomenological approaches to social life…are endeavours to understand how the world is perceived and understood from the points of view of particular individuals and groups'. How do they 'see, perceive, understand, experience, make sense of, respond to, emotionally feel about and engage with particular objects and circumstances' (2019: 78). Perceptions, experiences and understandings allow, and are shaped by, the unconscious or semi-conscious, habitual actions and interactions of people in daily life.

Thought about the relationship between our perception of the world and how our minds work is part of a phenomenological tradition of German philosophy going back to Immanuel Kant on human consciousness in general, and developed further in the works of Edmund Husserl and sociologists in the nineteenth and early twentieth centuries. But the most important figures in the development of twentieth-century **phenomenology** were the German philosopher Martin Heidegger and the French philosopher Maurice Merleau-Ponty. Heidegger's publications, most famously *Being and Time* (1962), have undoubtedly influenced many of the European social scientists and poststructuralists cited in Chapter 4, but they have also given rise to caustic commentary among some readers: Inwood (2019: 1) calls him 'the greatest charlatan ever to claim the title of philosopher, a master of hollow verbiage masquerading as profundity' and *Being and Time* 'one of the most difficult books every written' (2019: 14) – and that is up against some pretty stiff competition! Understanding is not helped by the fact that what Heidegger published in this book was only about one-third of the book that he had planned to publish. More controversial was Heidegger's anti-semitism and committed membership of the Nazi party. On the right of the modern political spectrum his influence stretches to Steve Bannon and prominent groups of neo-fascists. As such this raises questions about the importance of people's politics in our assessment of how to work with their ideas (Thomas 1996: 2–3).

Heidegger's thought has been particularly influential in a variety of disciplines, including archaeology and anthropology, since the early 1990s. His central idea was expressed in the word 'Dasein', translated into English as 'Being-in-the-world'. The world in which we, as beings, live includes people, objects and what is usually called the environment, but this is not an external, natural world that surrounds, and is separate from, that of human beings. We are not active cultural 'subjects' in contrast to passive, animate or inanimate natural 'objects'. Individual experience is seen through people's different cultures and the everyday world views (or 'lifeworlds') that they share with each other and take for granted in their everyday actions. This 'dwelling' in the world creates and is based on relationships between people, places and things which have histories and memories seen and symbolised in their locations. This perception and experience was, perhaps not surprisingly, pursued through the senses of the human body (we see, hear, smell, taste and touch objects and people in the world around us), although Heidegger says little directly about this. The skills that we have learned or been taught, including how to make use of material 'things', are 'lived' and repeated during our everyday, routine, activities. This everyday knowledge of the world has greater subjectivity, given that individuals' perceptions of the world stem from their 'lifeworlds' and the particular times in which they live. Merleau-Ponty built on Heidegger's arguments against the separation of mind and body and for a central study of how our bodies dwell in 'lived space' and engage with the world through our senses, most notably in his book *Phenomenology of Perception* (1962). He devoted much greater attention to this bodily engagement than did Heidegger.

While the works of Heidegger and Merleau-Ponty were influential in the presentation and adoption of the kinds of ideas about place, memory and agency presented in Chapter 4, phenomenology did not begin to make its impact on archaeology in the UK until the 1990s. This was partly through reading of the works of the anthropologist Tim Ingold (e.g. 1993, 2000). Chris Gosden (1994) presented a theory on social change and social being. Julian Thomas (1996: 234) followed Heidegger's central argument that 'human beings become aware of themselves and their surroundings in the context of everyday life: we find ourselves in the course of living'. He redefined culture as 'a means of human engagement with the world' (236) using the skills learned in everyday life, while embedding the production and change in meaning and symbolism of culture through this human being in the world. In essence, he offered us 'an exercise in working out what a Heideggerian archaeology might look like' (1996: 2) in three case studies from Neolithic Britain. Chris Tilley's (1994) phenomenology of landscape was particularly influential in the study of Neolithic monuments and landscapes in the UK (Box 5.2). Tilley's landscape studies became the subject of criticism and debate. For example, was the analysis based on coherent methodology that could be checked by other archaeologists? How did site preservation and landscape changes affect our perception of landscapes? How far were Tilley's (and others') experiences of Neolithic landscapes based on the assumption of some kind of universal human body ('the white, heterosexual, modern male' as Brück (2005: 59) put it), failing to recognise the effect differences of culture, gender, class, education, sight, etc., on our perceptions of the world around us. How subjective were the observations made by individual observations in landscapes? More broadly, these examples of phenomenological archaeology were charged with having too great a focus on sight in perception (see Hamilakis 2013). This leads to the broadest question of all: is human life solely a sensual experience? What about our daily social, political and economic lives and the larger-scale structures of human societies (see Chapters 2–4), or must our concern with these be consigned to the dustbin of theories past?

BOX 5.2 EXPERIENCING THE LANDSCAPE

What is 'landscape'? Drawing on the founding fathers of phenomenology, the phenomenological school of geography, and ethnographic analogies from indigenous societies such as Australian Aborigines, Tilley answers this question by dismissing the notion that it is a 'neutral background' to human social life. It is not 'nature' as opposed to 'culture'. The world around us has shaped and been shaped by human action from the time of our earliest ancestors. The landscape is of the living and the dead. It has been exploited for all kinds of material and symbolic resources. For the Australian Aborigines, for example, 'the landscape is ... filled with meaning and memories, redolent of the actions of the past. The ancestral beings fixed in the land itself, in the trees, hills, lakes, sand-dunes and water-courses, become timeless reference points for the living' (1994: 41). During the course of daily 'dwelling' (e.g. walking along paths, building) a landscape 'is lived in and through, mediated, worked on and altered, replete with cultural meaning and symbolism – and not just something looked at or thought about' (1994: 26). People, through the senses of their bodies, experience and understand the world around them. Pathways and places such as monuments 'orchestrate human experience' (Bradley 1993: 48).

Tilley studies two ways in which landscapes are 'enculturated': through the meanings and memories given to places such as caves, rock shelters, sand-dunes, cliff bases, and to the appropriation of such ancestral meanings, memories and powers in the human construction of monuments in the creation of their social identities and biographies. His study focuses on the Mesolithic and Neolithic periods in three areas of southern Britain, namely, Pembrokeshire, the Black Mountains and Cranborne Chase. His interest is in experiencing what it is like to be in these landscapes. For example, what patterns of visibility and intervisibility are there between sites, from how far away can they be seen, and which paths of movement can be followed through the landscape? Perhaps the best example is his walking of the Neolithic Dorset Cursus on Cranborne Chase (1994: 170–200).

Among his later experiences of sites and landscapes, Tilley (2004: 87–145) traces the development of prehistoric Maltese 'temples' and shows how their architectural design had intended effects in relation to their bodily experience: for example, the designs caused changes in body posture, visibility, smell and sound when walking through the temples, as well as manipulation of spatial perspectives (2004: 131–3). Experience of spaces within the temples was intentionally controlled.

As we will see, Heidegger has also been influential in the comparatively recent development of relational thought in archaeology. For now, it is important to note that archaeology, as well as other social sciences, has largely embraced the idea that we live in and through our bodies. We are material and cultural beings. How we perceive the world through our senses is shaped by our cultural contexts and daily practices. We are embodied and we experience the world through our **embodiment** (see Meskell 1999: 37–8). The authors in Robb and Harris (2013) present examples of embodied thinking and practices from prehistoric and historic periods, including stone-working technologies in the Lower Palaeolithic, the effects of economic change (in this case, the adoption of agriculture in the Neolithic) on the body (e.g. stature, diet, disease loads), and how class divisions and aspirations were embodied in the idealised representation of the body in Classical Greek sculptures.

PERSONHOOD

But who are these embodied beings? They may have individual bodies (what Meskell 1999: 32 calls the 'skin-bound mortal human being'), but does that mean that they were individual persons? Is the concept of the individual, as we use it today, applicable to human beings and societies in the past (Box 4.2)? Once again, these questions challenge us to think differently about our ancestors and not simply to project our bodies and the ways in which we think about ourselves and our lives into culturally different pasts. As Harris and Cipolla (2017: 61) point out, in the modern West we see ourselves as unique 'bounded individuals', persons with our individual names, nuclear families, genders (either male or female) ascribed from birth, personal possessions, and even individual bedrooms. Our personal identities (see Chapter 4) are built on these characteristics, along with those of our ethnicity, class, religion, and so on, although these characteristics are not necessarily static during our lifetimes (e.g. changes in gender, income group). We are defined as individual persons in human societies, separate from animals and things in and around our worlds.

This way of thinking about ourselves and our **personhood** (what Fowler 2004: 7 calls 'the state or condition of being a person') is argued not to be universal: for example, in the British Isles, there is historical evidence that it was not present before the late seventeenth century, while ethnographic analogies from areas like Melanesia, southern India and Mesoamerica suggest the existence of different concepts and forms of personhood. As the anthropologist Marilyn Strathern argues, the people of Melanesia do not think of themselves primarily as 'bounded' individuals 'that entered into relationships (with the world, each other and so on) but rather emerge out of these relationships' (Harris and Cipolla 2017: 63). These social relationships are with their contemporaries, their ancestors, and their environments (e.g. animals, plants, rivers, objects of all kinds). People's identities are 'composite' and change with changes in these relationships. As Fowler (2004: 26) puts it, Melanesian people are 'multiply-authored', that is, 'each person encompasses multiple constituent things and relations received from other people'. They are 'dividuals' rather than 'individuals'. For example, when Melanesian people initiate social relationships with each other, they exchange objects or animals. Such objects (e.g. arm shells) may be worn on the body and might be argued to be visible symbols of these relationships. But they are also part of the identity of the donor, which has now been transferred in part to the receiver. A further contrast to Western beliefs and practices is that objects in Melanesia are also thought to be persons. For example, the Sabarl people on the island of New Britain attribute a life force to axes and name different

---

BOX 5.3 FRAGMENTATION AND PERSONHOOD

If objects were used to create relationships and composite identities, then this could be done with either whole or fragmentary examples, and on death those objects could be appropriated by other members of the community to change their composite identities? It is blindingly obvious to anyone with a basic grasp of archaeology that so much of the material that we find in the ground is in pieces. Why that should be the case is another matter. The common cultural or social reasons given for this fragmentation include accidental breakage and subsequent discard (i.e. 'rubbish'), ritual 'killing', and ritual disposal in what are called 'structured deposits' (Chapman 2000: 23–7). But could this fragmentation of objects have been intentional and central to social practices for the creation of relationships and identities? In a detailed study of the fragmentation, distribution and depositional contexts of later prehistoric objects in south-eastern Europe, Chapman (2000: 23–48)) argues that there are two general ways in which objects play important roles in social relations: enchainment (effectively connecting people through 'chains' of fragmented objects and thereby maintaining their shared identities and more equal access to valued objects) and accumulation (the appropriation of intact objects in groups, such as in graves and hoards, by individuals or groups of people within communities). Over a period of several thousand years, relations of accumulation became more important than those of enchainment and a different kind of personhood emerged in south-eastern Europe. Fowler (2004) cites other archaeological case studies of how the concept of personhood can be useful, for example, in the study of the treatment of the human body after death in the Bronze Age and how Late Bronze Age swords were conceived as persons.

parts of them after different parts of the human body. The Melanesian ethnographies of Strathern and other anthropologists exerted a strong influence on archaeologists in the early 2000s (Box 5.3).

While the concept of personhood has been picked up by a variety of (especially British) archaeologists, it has also been the subject of criticism. Great weight was initially placed on ethnographic analogies derived from Melanesia. Spriggs (2008) argues that the direct and uncritical use of all such analogies overlooks the ways in which societies studied by anthropologists have been changed by European contact and colonialism. Rather than taking analogies out of their historical contexts and applying them to the European Neolithic and Bronze Ages, we should be comparing historical sequences of cultural change between Pacific and European regions. Jones (2005) criticises the over-reliance by archaeologists on the Melanesian notion of personhood (e.g. what about notions of personhood in areas like Mesoamerica and Peru?) producing a generalised picture of the European Neolithic (2005: 194). Among other criticisms, Brittain and Harris (2010) raise doubts about the reliability of the patterns defined for south-eastern Europe by Chapman and argue that different forms of personhood are visible in both anthropological and archaeological contexts. One important outcome of these critiques is an agreement that 'personhood is historically and socially contingent' and 'discussions of personhood have also done much to spearhead the broader focus on thinking about the past in terms of relations' (Harris and Cipolla 2017: 66).

RELATIONAL THINKING

Debates about dualisms, materiality, embodiment, phenomenology and personhood, stimulated by study of indigenous societies and knowledge systems, are examples of how we can think in very different ways about ourselves and our pasts. This change in thinking in archaeology was given a further impetus at the dawn of the new millennium by the appearance of a suite of theoretical ideas from Continental philosophy about the nature of reality and our place in the world. These ideas are difficult to subsume within a single '-ism' or theory: you will find reference to speculative realism, object-oriented philosophies, agential realism, flat ontologies, and posthumanism, as well as Actor-Network Theory, Assemblage

Thought and Thing Theory (Table 5.2; Bryant *et al.* 2011; Thomas 2015). This range of philosophical approaches is grouped together in the literature as marking a '**Speculative Turn**', a '**Material Turn**' ('**New Materialisms**') or an '**Ontological Turn**' in the humanities and social sciences.

The 'ontological' focus of these approaches concerns the nature of reality, of being and the concepts with which we think about and understand the human and non-human entities that exist in that material world. The 'material' part revisits the nature and properties of materials, the roles that they play in the human world, and the interrelationships of human and non-human entities. For example, the political scientist Jane Bennett (2010: vii) took aim at the distinction that is often made between the 'vibrant' life of human beings and the 'dull', 'raw, brute and inert' nature of matter, drawing on a tradition of thought from Democritus to Latour and Deleuze (see below) that stressed what she calls 'thingly power', that is, 'the curious ability of inanimate things to animate, to act, to produce effects dramatic and subtle' (2010: 6).

Common to all these theories, approaches, and -'isms' is what is called a 'relational' approach. This is defined by Matthew Johnson (2020: 146) as follows:

> A relational view criticizes the general belief that the world consists of detached, definite things, substances, elements, and that agency

Table 5.2 New materialisms, key authors and their disciplines

Actor Network Theory:	Bruno Latour (Sociology)
Posthumanism:	Rosa Braidotti (Feminist Critical Theory)
Agential Realism:	Karen Barad (Quantum Physics)
Assemblage Thought:	Gilles Deleuze (Philosophy)
	Felix Guattari (Psychoanalysis)
	Manuel DeLanda (Philosophy)
	Jane Bennett (Political Science)
Thing Theory:	Bill Brown (American literature)
Object-Oriented Ontologies:	Graham Harman (Philosophy)
Speculative Realism:	Levi Bryant (Philosophy)
	Graham Harman (Philosophy)
Flat Ontologies:	Ian Bogost (Media Studies)

can be assigned to some of these things and not others. Instead, a relational view stresses the interdependence and mutual constitution of things. Things, humans, animals, landscapes, only come into being in relation to each other; they have no prior existence independent of each other. In a relational view, these connections and mutual dependencies are often seen as fluid and constantly changing.

To quote Thomas (1996: 236) 'history is a lived process in which relationships between human beings and their world are continually transformed'. This way of thinking challenged many of the basic theoretical ideas that we have examined in Chapters 2–4. Given that there are now whole books devoted to relational approaches in archaeology (e.g. Watts 2013b; Jervis 2019; Alt and Pauketat 2020; Crellin 2020; Crellin *et al.* 2021), what follows is a selective presentation of the most cited approaches introduced into archaeology, their protagonists, and examples of their applications.

ACTOR-NETWORK 'THEORY'

The Frenchman Bruno Latour describes himself as an 'anthropologist of science and technology', although others have called him 'an empirical philosopher', or a 'sociologist'. He started his career in the 1970s making detailed studies of how scientists worked and how they constructed scientific facts, by observing scientists in laboratories. Rather than imagining scientists, 'discovering' facts just by using equipment and carrying out standardised experiments, Latour (1987) followed through all stages of science from such experiments, including the 'translation' of observations into tables, figures and charts, and the publication of results). In a standard account, the 'actors' doing science would be individual, conscious scientists, but Latour introduced the term '**actant**' to refer to these scientists, as well as to the non-human things like machines or instruments, objects being studied and notebooks. He defined an actant as 'something that acts or to which activity is granted by others', implying 'no special motivation of human actors', and being 'anything provided it is granted to be the source of an action' (cited in Inglis and Thorpe 2019: 250). In contrast to the individual agency possessed by humans (see Chapter 4), Latour's actants act within the context of relationships within networks.

This weighting given both to humans and non-humans takes agency beyond the argument produced by the British anthropologist Alfred Gell (clearly summarised by Harris and Cipolla 2017: 73–7), who distinguished between 'primary agents' (human beings endowed with the capacity for intentional action) and 'secondary agents' (objects, artefacts, for example, your laptop computer) 'through which 'primary' agents distribute their agency'.

For Latour the material world made no distinction between humans and non-humans, or between human beings and a natural world, and in any analysis, they were treated as of equal weight, or 'symmetrically' as he put it. This did not imply that humans and non-humans had exactly the same capabilities, simply that human beings did not have a prior, dominant role in the material world (**anthropocentrism**). Both humans and non-humans had the ability to act in the world, not on their own but in relation to each other. This argument was an essential part of what became known from the 1980s as **actor-network theory** (ANT). Latour kept it even though he thought it was wrongly named: 'There are four things that do not work with actor-network theory; the word actor, the word network, the word theory and the hyphen!' (cited in de Vries 2016: 15). ANT was internally debated and changed over time, and emphasis was placed on detailed description rather than explanation, more method than theory. Latour's ambition was not to create a sociological theory but to create a different social science, 'a technique for describing the social world' (de Vries 2016: 88), which redefined the meaning of being human. This social science was expressed through a string of new concepts.

In addition to dualisms such as human/non-human and structure-agency, ANT (discussed in detail in Latour 2005) rejected the abstract concepts of social theory (see Chapters 2 and 4) such as 'society', 'social structure' and 'social system, as well as what many social scientists see as the dynamic of social change between small-scale social relations and larger-scale social structure': 'the social is not made up of structure and agency….(but) made out of circulations of all kinds of actants' (Inglis and Thorpe 2019: 249), that is, networks, or 'collectives', of human and non-human entities. Specific networks shape the characteristics of these entities and they are inherently open to change. The arrangement of these entities in networks also shapes the nature of social power.

For example, the way in which the mercantile state of Portugal in the fifteenth and sixteenth centuries A.D. expanded into a viable, global empire depended on the creation of networks of both human and non-human actants: these included people such as sailors, soldiers and ship-builders, and the technical knowledge (e.g. navigation, map making) and devices (e.g. deep-sea boats, astrolobes) needed to overcome the challenges of specific, long-distance voyages. 'The network that the Portuguese human actors constructed can be seen not just as *part* of their empire, but rather as their empire *as such*: the 'empire' *was* the network and vice-versa' (Inglis and Thorpe 2019: 257).

Such interrelated networks of human beings, animals, plants and material objects/things are based on what is called a **flat ontology**. The archaeologist Rachel Crellin (2020: 160–1) describes working with a flat ontology, what it is and especially what it is not, as follows:

> I am not arguing that we live in a world where cars, shoes, people, and iguanas are all equally important and powerful. Nor is it about saying that in the pasts that I study pots, cremations, bronze axes, people and seeds are all equally important or powerful. Rather, it is about saying that all these different protagonists are *equally capable* of having an effect in our world.

We start with the assumption of a flat ontology when we study change and the human role in it.

Criticisms of ANT (e.g. Inglis and Thorpe 2019: 259–63) have ranged from the ways in which its central argument downplays the distinctive nature of human qualities, to its 'clever word-play and confusing terminologies', its brushing aside of the value of abstract social concepts like class, the reduction of everything to descriptive networks, and its fragmented development from the 1980s to the 1990s. But ANT has been widely influential in the social sciences, especially on studies of materiality (Knappett 2012: 192) and 'things' (see below). The anthropologist Tim Ingold has adopted a relational approach that cites a variety of influences, from Heidegger to Latour, citing indigenous knowledge systems attributing animacy to objects and personhood to human and non-human animals (1996: 129–36), as well as doubting the attribution of intentional agency to objects and arguing in favour of the concept of a 'meshwork' in contrast to Latour's 'network' (Ingold 2011: 63–5).

The publications of Latour and others in science studies have been widely cited in archaeology since the late 1990s, whether criticising the use of dualisms, discussing the creation of scientific knowledge and the construction of facts (e.g. Jones 2002: 29–37 on archaeological theory and scientific practice), the practices and 'theorising' of fieldwork (e.g. Lucas 2012: 222–57), assessing the utility of abstract concepts such as society, culture, economy, class and chiefdoms (e.g. Lucas 2012: 169–214), and developing a methodology for studying networks (e.g. Knappett 2011). In embracing ANT, archaeologists engaged with a challenge to the concept of agency and revisited the idea of 'active' material culture that was central to the postprocessual archaeology of the 1980s. The most direct influence of ANT has been seen in what is called '**symmetrical archaeology**' (Box 5.4). But we also have to ask ourselves, as archaeologists, whether Latour's ANT gives sufficient attention to historical processes of short- and long-term change (Crellin 2020: 151–2).

BOX 5.4 SYMMETRICAL ARCHAEOLOGY

Publications on symmetrical archaeology (SA) made their appearance in the first decade of the present century, most notably in the work of Michael Shanks, Chris Witmore, Timothy Webmoor and Bjorner Olsen. Shanks (2007: 591) tells us what he thinks SA is not: 'It is not a new theory. It is not another borrowed methodology', and 'it is not another -ism' for archaeologists to mimic' (594), while Witmore (2007: 547) argues that SA 'does not aim to establish itself as the latest paradigm shift'. Drawing on ANT and a range of influences from philosophy and science and technology studies, it shares Latour's rejection of dualisms (including that of structure and agency) and of abstract concepts of society and social relations, in favour of the symmetrical (but not equivalent) treatment of humans and non-humans in networks of relationships. A central concept in SA is that of 'things': 'all those enormously varied physical entities we by effective historic conventions refer to as "material culture" ... beings in the world alongside other beings such as humans, plants and animals' (Olsen 2012: 212).

Rather than being seen as representations of past societies and cultures, having symbolic and economic importance, valued for their meaning in human societies, things have their own embodied knowledge, skills and capacities and are 'entangled' (see below) with other things and physical entities. In other words, they are not 'means to reach something else that is more important: cultures and societies, or the lives of past peoples' (Olsen 2012: 219–20).

In SA archaeologists do not 'discover' the past, rather they work with 'remains' of that past. This practice requires networks of skilled people (e.g. excavators, specialists) and equipment (e.g. instruments and tools), as well as the process of 'translation' of material remains into the material past, or what is normally called the 'archaeological record' (e.g. through manual and digital recording practices). Things are entangled in networks of people and things (see Olsen *et al.* 2012: 58–135). But it is also important to note that 'pasts are not exclusively past. Something of the past exists in the here and now' (Witmore 2007: 556). Olsen *et al.* (2012: 136–56) give an instructive case study from the Argive Plain in Greece of how the pasts that exist at any one time are 'multiple' pasts, while Witmore (2007: 556) shows how the lives of modern communities and people in some areas of Western Europe are shaped by Roman road networks.

Harris and Cipolla (2017: 138) make a distinction between two phases in SA's development: a 'first wave' primarily following Latour's lead, and a 'second wave' more influenced by the philosopher Graham Harman, placing greater emphasis on the importance of 'things' and arguably less concerned with the past.

HUMANISM, POSTHUMANISM AND POSTCOLONIALISM

In rejecting anthropocentrism, Latour rejected the notion that the motor of change in the world was provided exclusively by human agency, as active, animate subjects dominated inert, inanimate objects. More broadly, this was a rejection of the concept of 'human exceptionalism': Bennett (2010: 34) describes this as 'the human tendency to underestimate the degree to which people, animals, artifacts, technologies and elemental forces share powers and operate in dissonant conjunction with each other'.

Human 'exceptionalism' was central to the dualism claimed between culture and nature, and along with human nature, agency, rationality, individual liberty and respect for evidence in coming to judgments about the world around us, is a key part of a broader way of thought known as **humanism** (itself closely aligned to Modernism) in the Western world. Humanism put humans in the place of God at the centre of the universe. As Watts (2013b: 3) puts it, 'only humans are capable of knowing the world, abstractly and assuredly, through acts of consciousness', giving meaning to all parts of the material world.

It will come as no surprise that the most critical response to humanism is known as **posthumanism**, which draws on a range of theoretical positions, from poststructuralism and feminism to postcolonialism. In contrast to anthropocentrism, the world is composed of networks/collectives of human beings, animals, plants and material objects. It is the effects, not any intentions, of these entities that are active in change in the world. Take one example, Charles Darwin's study of English worms (cited in Bennett 2010: 95–8) concluded that they are important in world history, making topsoil, enabling and supporting growth of all kinds of edible plants, covering and preserving human activities and materials: 'worms protect "for an indefinitely long period every object, not liable to decay, which is dropped on the surface of the land, by burying it beneath their castings"'. As Bennett (2010: 96) puts it, the worm's contribution to history is 'the unplanned result of worms acting in conjunction and competition with other (biological, bacterial, chemical, human) agents'.

Criticisms of humanism, including its rationality and placing of human beings at the centre of history can be seen in poststructuralist thought from the late 1960s onwards (Braidotti 2013: 16–25). The assumption that these human beings were male, white, urbanised and heterosexual (Braidotti 2013: 65) was an important object of feminist and queer theory critique in the following decades. From the nineteenth century, non-white, indigenous peoples of the non-Western world provided analogies for the cultures, societies and subsistence practices of the West's 'primitive' ancestors. They were 'people without history'. Their so-called 'primitiveness' was also used as a justification for Western colonialism and imperialism. How we view indigenous peoples and understand their knowledge systems, let alone bring them into the study of their own histories, has been given a major boost by **postcolonial theory**, which was developed in literary criticism by scholars such as Edward Said, Gayatri Spivak and Homi Bhabha. Their starting point can be seen in Said's (1978) attack on Western scholarship's perception of the Eastern world (essentially backward and without history). Instead of being the objects of study, non-Western scholars now rejected Eurocentric understandings of their societies, studying continuity and change in their world from their own perspectives, especially in the context of the interactions that took place between those who colonised and those who were colonised. The colonised now had voices.

Although postcolonial theory was being developed from the late 1970s, it was not until the turn of the millennium that it began to be adopted into archaeology in the form of what are called 'Postcolonial' or 'Indigenous' Archaeologies. As Gosden (2012: 252–3) emphasises, this does not mark the establishment of a 'single, sub-field of the discipline, but a series of overlapping areas' with critical study of the histories of colonialism and the interaction of colonialism and the practice of archaeology. He also cautions that 'we are travelling towards a post-colonial archaeology rather than having arrived there' (2012: 259). One of the most productive dynamics has been between indigenous peoples in general, as well as those trained as archaeologists, and Western archaeologists, in the setting of research agendas, the pursuit of fieldwork projects and, most contentious of all, the curation of human remains and material culture (see Box 4.1) (Colwell-Chanthaphonh 2012; Bruchac *et al.* 2010). Rather than one tradition of Indigenous thought, there is much variation in how, for example, peoples in areas such as the Pacific and North America, understand the worlds around them. As Lindsay Montgomery (2021: 57) puts it, 'the existence of over 5,000 distinct indigenous nations worldwide suggests that characterizing an "Indigenous" theoretical approach, even if restricted to the 573 federally recognized Tribal Nations within the United States, is empirically tenuous'. Given this variation, it is important to grasp the different impacts of colonialism on different indigenous peoples and communities. Also important is to focus greater attention to the weight we give to indigenous (e.g. oral traditions), as opposed to Western ways of knowing the present and past worlds. Although this interaction has been perceived as a struggle between 'traditions' and 'science', the best examples of practice show that this is a false dualism (e.g. examples in Silliman 2008; Bruchac *et al.* 2010; Atalay 2012; Colwell-Chanthaphonh 2012).

'Other' ways of thinking about the world have a long history of indigenous practice and anthropological study, especially within the content of what have been called 'religious' beliefs. To the Western eye, these beliefs seem strange and hard to accept, given that they challenge the boundaries between humans, animals, plants and 'things' in general. This is especially the case when animals are given what we regard as human characteristics, such as an inner essence or soul (e.g. Harris and Cipolla 2017: 180–5 on **animism**), but with different bodily forms. The human–animal boundaries have also been blurred by the biologist Donna Haraway's (e.g. 2003) study of the mutual relationships between animals and humans: even though these relationships are asymmetric (we domesticate cats/dogs), animals can (in the popular phrase) 'bite back', that is, their actions shape our behaviour. Once again, this blurs boundaries between humans and non-human animals and weakens, it is argued, the case for anthropocentrism.

ASSEMBLAGE THOUGHT

Assemblage thought has recently become influential in archaeology (e.g. Jervis 2019). Its most-cited sources are the works of the poststructuralist philosopher Giles Deleuze (in collaboration with the psychoanalyst Felix Guattari) and the Mexican philosopher Manuel DeLanda. If Heidegger's *Being and Time* is a challenging read, then up there with it is Deleuze and Guattari's *A Thousand Plateaus* (1987), a book on the history of capitalism. Deleuze and Guattari's thinking, like Latour's, comes with their own (in some cases multisyllabic) neologisms, and they even give different definitions of assemblages in the same volume. The key ideas and concepts of assemblage thought are presented in a much more accessible way, although not always agreeing with Deleuze and Guattari, by DeLanda (2016). He also referred to assemblage theory rather than thought, a promotion that is debated.

Assemblage thought is similar to ANT in its posthumanism, relationality and flat ontology. There are different definitions of what an assemblage is, but the clearest is given by Harris and Cipolla (2017:

139): 'an assemblage is the coming together of things into what we can consider a single whole. These include materials, but also ideas, beliefs, emotions, memories, symbols and more'. Immediately, you can see why the concept of an assemblage is often used interchangeably with Latour's 'network' and Ingold's 'meshwork', although these concepts and their workings are not identical: for example, Latour's networks are comprised of actants, as opposed to the 'components' of DeLanda's assemblages. Overall assemblages occur at different scales in time and space, with different degrees of coherence, and in different historical contexts. Even the world is an assemblage. At a much smaller scale, Crellin (2020: 165) uses the everyday example of a vegetable patch as an assemblage, with its soil, plants, compost, weeds, seeds, insects, etc. However keen the gardener, an annual yield depends not only on the possession of green fingers but also on the relations between all of the patch's components. The 'gathering' (a concept that originated with Heidegger) together of these components, each of which comprises its own assemblage (e.g. the plants with their component parts), is temporary (e.g. different plants may be cultivated in successive years; the vegetable patch may be turfed over or 'wilded' when it becomes too much work for the ageing owners). Assemblages and relations between them are never fixed, but always 'becoming', and elements within assemblages may be detached from their setting and attached to another assemblage (what is called 'exteriority'). There are no single causes or directions of change, which can be sudden and unpredictable. Change is not the exclusive outcome of human agency, but of the relationships between the components, including humans, of individual assemblages. These relationships are important in ensuring that the assemblages are more than the sum of their parts. The archaeologist Ben Jervis (2019: 37–47) gives an introduction to all the key, theoretical concepts.

Two of the key concepts are 'territorialisation' and 'deterritorialisation', exemplified in Ruth Van Dyke's study of urbanism in Chaco Canyon in the American Southwest (Box 5.5). Other studies on the urban assemblages in the past include those presented in Alt and Pauketat (2020), and in Jervis's (2016) work on medieval England. Harris (2013) takes an assemblage approach to Neolithic and Early Bronze Age communities in Britain, shows the complex Bronze Age communities in Britain, and shows the complex interplay of the processes of territorialisation and deterritorialisation in the bringing together and dispersal of communities. Other studies have focussed on the 'gathering' together of burial assemblages containing different components, with different histories and places of origin: for example, some pots deposited with the dead may have been specially produced for interment, while others were part of assemblages of living communities. Jervis (2019: 48–54) gives the example of grave no. 20, from the Anglo-Saxon cemetery at Great Chesterford, in which a variety of grave goods (assemblages in themselves) were brought together, in the process of territorialisation, to construct a specific burial assemblage. More examples of assemblage thought in archaeology can be found in Jervis (2019: 30–2) and Crellin (2020: 167–8).

BOX 5.5 ASSEMBLAGE THOUGHT AND CHACO CANYON

Chaco Canyon is a famous location for archaeological research in the American Southwest. From the mid-ninth to the mid-tenth centuries A.D., there emerged an urban landscape of both small and monumental sites linked by roads and occupied by up to around 6,000 people. Beyond the canyon, Chacoan sites, architecture and materials were distributed over an area of at least 60,000 square miles. The emergence of the Chacoan has mainly been understood through social, political and economic and religious/ceremonial interpretations. In contrast, Van Dyke (2020: 40) adopts an assemblage approach to cities in general, defining them as 'gatherings, places where buildings, people, materials, activities, experiences, and memories overlap and intertwine with a density that defies disentanglement'. More succinctly, she describes Chaco as 'a place that gathers people and topography, sensory experience and ancestral connections' (2020: 41).

Van Dyke focuses on two of Deleuze and Guattari's key concepts: territorialising processes (e.g. bringing together and keeping people, animals, materials and places in an urban assemblage) and deterritorialising processes pulling them apart. These processes are not exclusive (that is, one following the other), as 'assemblages are simultaneously, constantly, multidimensionally pulling (and being pulled), pushing (and being pushed), gathering (and being gathered), resisting (and being resisted)' (2020: 44). She describes these processes through study of the place that comprises Chaco Canyon, the experiences (through the human body) of making and being in these places, and the historical relationships of time, memory and ancestors in these places. For example, the place includes the landforms and their histories of ancestors and deities; the construction, distribution, planning and orientations of buildings and monuments; and water and agricultural production, with intertwined assemblages of corn growing and its processing and consumption. Territorialising processes included 'the gathering of buildings and labor, through cosmological symbolism and bodily experience, agricultural practices and the nurturing of life' (2020: 49), while deterritorialising processes may have included factors such as environmental instability, topography, distance and social relations.

While assemblage thought bears noticeable similarities to Latour's conception of networks, its proponents also argue that there are significant differences: for example, Crellin (2020: 151–2)) argues that Latour and ANT do not provide the kind of approach to historical stability and change that is required in archaeology. Harris (2018: 97) is sufficiently confident of the strength of assemblage thought that he refers to a 'Deleuzian archaeology', suggests that 'at its heart is the connection between history and materiality' and that this makes it 'a new historical materialism, one that points to how differing forms of material relationships allow different kinds of history to emerge'. This is a bold claim to make, but as we shall, there is an equally bold claim made for entanglement theory.

ENTANGLEMENT THEORY

The concept and approach of **entanglement** in archaeology are most closely associated with Ian Hodder (e.g. 2012c, 2018), who draws on contemporary studies of the relationships between people and **things** (Box 5.6) in archaeology, the humanities and the social sciences. These 'roots' of entanglement (Der and Fernandini 2016: 12–18) include the works and ideas of the main proponents of networks, meshworks, materiality, and material engagement. The concept 'entanglement' was present in an influential book by anthropologist Nicholas Thomas (1991). Hodder also draws on Heidegger's ideas on things and on humans 'being-in-the-world', rather than existing separately from the world and all the

---

BOX 5.6 THINGS, OBJECTS AND ARTEFACTS

The last two decades have witnessed renewed interest in 'things', or what a historian has called 'the material stuff of life' (Trentmann 2009: 283), across the humanities and social sciences. There is even a branch of study called 'Thing Theory' (Brown 2001). But what are things? In some contexts, the concept is used ambiguously or without definition, as in our own societies. Compare the question 'What is that thing over there?' and the viewpoint that 'things are not what they used to be': in the first case the thing is a physical entity, but in the second one it suggests more a condition of life experience in the present (e.g. politics, health provision, popular music). 'Things' may be used interchangeably with 'objects' (Harman's 2010 object-oriented ontology) and 'artefacts', often used without definition. For Bennett (2010: 6), things are non-human and inanimate matter, as they are for Actor Network Theory and Symmetrical Archaeology: for Olsen (2010) things have individual qualities (e.g. handmade pots have a wide variety of forms, sizes, clays and tempers). 'Things include big objects (trains, cities, planets), soft things (butter, cotton, sponges), small artifacts coins, pearls, microchips), durable matter (stones, rocks, iron) and perishable goods (bread, leaves, dew)' (Olsen 2010: 157). They may be specialised or multifunctional, and they are all material, although clearly, this does not imply that they do not also have symbolic meanings. To make matters more complicated, it is argued that there are different kinds of things, including 'ideas, beliefs, emotions, memories, symbols and more' (Harris and Cipolla 2017: 139) and things and humans cannot be separated from each other. In entanglement theory Hodder (2012c: 15) clearly defines 'thing' to refer to 'solid entities made or used by humans' and 'material entities that have an object nature', so have that in mind as you read this section.

species of plants and animals around them (2012c: 27–9). Neat dualisms such as culture/biology are rejected, especially given recent research in genetics and the development of the Extended Evolutionary Synthesis (Hodder 2018: 40–4). Hodder's focus on long-term stability and change in the past also leads him to explore evolutionary theory and to ask two big questions: 'Does human evolution have a direction? If so, why?'. But before we can reach for the sky and try to answer these questions, we need to know what entanglement is.

Hodder's argument begins by drawing our attention to the dependence of humans on things of all kinds (2012c: 15–39). This dependence on 'material stuff' has increased through human evolution and accelerated with consumerism. When we think about the things that we make or use, they enable us to live our daily lives, to reproduce ourselves both biologically and socially, to work, to relax, to interact with our fellow humans and so on. But this dependence on things also has a constraint, what Hodder calls 'dependency', that arises from the interaction between humans and things (e.g. addictions): At the same time, things depend on other things (2012c: 40–63). 'Any thing is dependent on the other things used to make it, to use it, to repair it, to discard it' (2012c: 47): the things and processes used to make a fire, or make and use wall plaster illustrate this interdependency. The chemical and physical properties of the raw materials and their finished products can enable ('afford') their potential for use: for example, the properties of different clays, along with added tempers and firing conditions may enable or constrain their use for different functions. Things also depend on humans (2012c: 64–87). In the case of animal domestication, there emerged a dependence on humans for factors such as animal maintenance and reproduction. Humans also became constrained by both animal and plant dependency: 'humans found themselves involved in tilling, watering, burning, clearing land, sowing, and transplanting plants, or in taming, protecting, herding, culling, and selectively breeding animals' (2012c: 79–80). The daily lives of humans were irrevocably changed as a result of the dependence of plants and animals on them. Hodder's archaeological applications of entanglement theory are almost exclusively based on his major excavations at Catalhoyuk (e.g. on the complex entanglements of clay in the early occupation of the site, 2012c: fig.9).

The relations of dependence and dependency between humans and things, things and other things, things and humans, and humans and humans are ones of 'entanglement'. These developing, increasingly complex, relations see humans entangled and 'entrapped' or 'locked' into what Hodder calls path dependent sequences of change (2012c: 105) (Box 5.7).

For Hodder (2018), human evolution does have a direction and it is towards greater and greater dependence on things and more extensive and complex entanglements with them. This understanding is preferred to ideas of human progress, or exclusively social or biological evolution. Rather than a dualism between culture and biology, the interactions between them are so extensive and deep-rooted that 'the cultural, the social, and the material enter directly into biological processes and vice versa' (2018: 40) – they are all entangled together. This entanglement is the motor of human

---

BOX 5.7 PATH DEPENDENCE

Hohokam irrigation in the American Southwest developed from the beginning of the first millennium to the middle of the second millennium A.D (Hegmon *et al.* 2016: 173–88). The Hohokam dug and maintained extensive canal systems, population sizes grew to a peak of some 50,000, regional systems of production and exchange developed and declined, and social hierarchies emerged. Hegmon *et al.* (2016: 173) argue that agricultural productivity, population size and density and the technology of canal construction, use and maintenance were increasingly entangled: for example, the food produced through irrigation could feed a larger population but this required a larger input of labour to dig and maintain the canal systems. At what point did the Hohokam become so 'locked-in' to irrigation agriculture that the population sizes and densities, coupled with their social and economic practices, could not exist without it? Hegmon *et al.* (2016: 178–81) answer this question by using data on the size and discharge of one of two canal systems in the Phoenix Basin to make calculations through time of the labour required to construct and maintain them, the acres being irrigated (and hence the crop production) and the population size that could be supported.

evolution. Once it takes a particular direction or path, it becomes difficult, if not impossible, to disentangle the entanglements.

As a relatively recent introduction to archaeology, entanglement has been both welcomed and criticised (see Crellin 2020: 148–50; and the debate in Hodder 2016: 129–50). Critical questions include:

1. How far is entanglement non-anthropocentric?
2. How far is disentanglement difficult or impossible?
3. Are Hodder's ideas of directionality and path dependence generalised from modern experience to a universal model of the entanglement of humans and things throughout time?
4. If we have the answer to the direction of human evolution, then what research about our long-term history is left to be done?
5. How far are interactions between humans and other humans qualitatively the same as those between humans and things, and between things and things?

To these questions may be added one about the status of the concept of entanglement. How far is it a theory that brings together a range of ideas drawn from different theoretical approaches, rather than a metaphor for thinking about the complex ways in which humans and things interact (Silliman 2016: 44)?

AND FINALLY

The relational archaeologies that have been developed since the 1990s present direct challenges to the theoretical approaches that dominated archaeological debates in the 1960–90s. Individual relational approaches, and criticisms of them, have been presented, and overall they raise two further questions. Do they signal the end of earlier theoretical approaches? Where are theory and archaeology going now and in the near future?

SUMMARY

• How can archaeologists study the past without projecting back the ways we think about the world around us as modern, Western human beings? In this chapter, we explore theoretical ideas that help us to think in different ways.

- Since the seventeenth century, we have perceived ourselves, and the world around us, in terms of polarised dualisms, for example, culture/nature, humans/animals, or mind/matter. This perception is heavily criticised.
- The concept of materiality helps us to think about the physicality of the material world and how this can enable and constrain human action. Making artefacts is a relationship between bodily skills and the properties of raw materials.
- Our engagement with the material world takes place through our senses, themselves part of the human body, which is both a social and a biological entity. The ways in which we perceive and understand the world have a long history of study through phenomenology. At the same time, questions are raised about the utility of the concept of human individuality and the nature of personhood.
- The turn of the millennium saw archaeology's adoption of new theories and ideas (e.g. actor network theory, flat ontologies, posthumanism, postcolonialism, assemblage thought and entanglement theory) drawn from the humanities and social sciences. These focussed on issues of ontology and were all examples of relational thinking. These approaches included criticism of human exceptionalism and anthropocentrism. They were also a challenge to many of the theoretical approaches in archaeology that have been presented in Chapters 2–4.

FURTHER READING

Harris and Cipolla (2017), Crellin (2020) and Johnson (2020: 132–55) are accessible introductions to relational archaeologies, while Watts (2013b) and Alt and Pauketat (2020) comprise wide-ranging case studies. Knappett (2012: 188–207) gives an informed and structured introduction to materiality. Inglis and Thorpe (2019: 79–98) and Zahavi (2019) present the basics of phenomenology. Tilley (1994) is a classic example of the phenomenology of landscape. A good introduction to thought about the human body is given by Shilling (2012), The contributors to Robb and Harris (2013) engage with the history of body theory from the Palaeolithic to the present day. Actor-Network Theory is presented by Inglis and Thorpe (2019: 244–64) and de Vries (2016), as is posthumanism by

Braidotti (2013). Harris and Cipolla (2017: 171–80) and Gosden (2012) do the same for postcolonial and indigenous archaeologies. Jervis (2019) presents assemblage thought in archaeology, and if you are of a philosophical bent, Colebrook (2002) on Deleuze is the book for you. Hodder (2012c and 2018) gives us the basic ideas of entanglement and its use in archaeology, while Der and Fernandini (2016) assemble a range of case studies from Europe, Asia and the New World.

WHERE NOW?

As the aim of this book is to provide a selective and simplified introduction to archaeological theory, then it is inevitable that there are approaches that have only been mentioned briefly or not at all (e.g. the archaeology of the contemporary era, Annales histories, social network analysis, complex systems). However, you have learned what theory is, and how it unites and divides archaeologists. The more explicit and detailed attention that is given to theory and theories has transformed archaeology during the last six decades. But how might archaeological theory develop in the 2020s? Any answer to this question will not be a prediction using a crystal ball, but proposing suggestions and questions based on the history and current state of archaeological theory.

LESSONS LEARNED

Let us begin with some of the important lessons we have learned about archaeological theory.

- Different theories enable us to ask different questions of our data. Marxism, Darwinism, Structuralism and so on are developing bodies of thought. Archaeologists have to understand the contents, nuances and contexts of these theories, and grasp how they may help us in practising archaeology. Our work is only just beginning when theories, let alone techniques, technologies and methodologies, are adopted in archaeology (Lucas 2015: 15–16).

DOI: 10.4324/9781315657097-6

- Different theories and types of archaeology (such as traditional, processual and postprocessual) have been changed by debate (what Hodder 2012b: 4 calls 'productive tensions'). They have within them the seeds of their own transformation, but they also respond to external changes in their wider disciplinary contexts. These theories and types of archaeology are also a form of individual and group identity, but the research directions of individual archaeologists, along with the theories on which they draw, often change through time.
- At any one time, there is always a diversity of theories in play. Such pluralism has been championed in the philosophy of science (e.g. Chang 2012: 270–8). Individual theories cannot answer all the questions we ask of our data, so we can profit from multiple lines of enquiry and competing interpretations. An over-emphasis on currently fashionable theories contributes to what is called 'disciplinary forgetting' (Jones 2009: 106).

GENERAL EXPECTATIONS?

We might expect that different theories will remain a feature of archaeology, but there will be cycles in their popularity (Kristiansen 2009). Experience will tell us when to reject theories that are reductionist (e.g. see Chapter 5 on theories that reduce the body to something that is either social or biological). Older and currently unfashionable theories will still generate useful data for archaeologists with different theoretical orientations. Archaeologists will continue to try and build bridges between different theories, but picking and mixing parts of different theories is not a risk-free strategy (e.g. how do you select these parts, are they compatible, do they lose some degree of meaning outside of their original contexts?). Different theories provide what McGuire (2008: 85) calls different 'entry points' to common subjects of interest (e.g. Marxist and feminist studies of social relations and exploitation). We will also continue to scan the intellectual horizons for theoretical developments in other disciplines. As Hodder (2012c: 222, citing the political scientist Shiping Tang) points out, 'however much theories in the social sciences aim to be comprehensive, there is always something left over, some awkwardness where the theory does not quite work, or some gaps that are unaddressed'. Individual theories are not theories of everything.

We need to understand older theories, as well as those that are currently popular, in order to grasp their contribution to the development of archaeological thought and the extent to which their relevance has been fully acknowledged. For example, Lycett and Shennan (2018) have returned to David Clarke's 1968 book *Analytical Archaeology* (a classic publication of processual archaeology, but almost never read today) to demonstrate its relevance to current Darwinian studies on cultural transmission. As we saw in Chapter 2, Marxism is far more nuanced than the dogmatic and deterministic theoretical approach that is often portrayed. It is also undeniable that key elements of postprocessualism (e.g. ideology, agency, the critique of knowledge of the past for its own sake) leaned heavily on Marxist thought. The concept of praxis has been widely accepted by archaeologists who would not necessarily regard themselves as Marxists (e.g. the range of contributors in Preucel and Mrozowski (2010)). Relational archaeologies (Chapter 5) also draw on elements of Marxism (e.g. materialist philosophy, praxis, approaches to power and ideology) (e.g. Crellin *et al.* 2021: 134–9). Both Marxist and Darwinian archaeologies are parts of long-standing, vibrant traditions of thought, with ongoing internal debates and varying popularities in different areas of the world: for example, Prentiss (2021) gives a succinct introduction to what she sees as the two major theoretical traditions, and their strengths and weaknesses, in evolutionary archaeology.

A NEW HISTORICAL MATERIALISM?

Archaeological theory seems to be changing markedly (see Chapter 5). Modernist perceptions of human beings and our worlds are a subject of criticism. As we have seen in Chapter 5, there are big claims to be putting in place a 'new historical materialism'. Is a fault line in archaeological theory emerging between relational approaches and existing archaeological theories? Do these approaches give us an agenda for archaeological theory for the next decade (Thomas 2015)?

It does not take a crystal ball to predict that relational approaches, with all their internal diversity, will continue to be practised and debated in archaeology. Although they have intellectual roots going back three decades, article and book length publications have accelerated in recent years. This upward trend will doubtless continue.

For some archaeologists, relational approaches are rather like a curate's egg, good in parts. On the positive side is the need to avoid projections of our Western cultural beliefs and practices into our study of the past. As we have seen, this has involved the use of ethnographic analogies (but still with the risk of taking them out of their historical contexts) and a more widespread development of indigenous and postcolonial archaeologies. Archaeological thought has also benefited from the criticisms of how we think of ourselves and the worlds in which we live through the use of polarised dualisms. Engagement with the politics of archaeology (e.g. whose interests are served by particular theoretical approaches?) is shared between relational and non-relational approaches.

Bigger challenges for contemporary theoretical archaeology are posed by posthumanism, flat ontologies and criticism of the kinds of abstract concepts on which a century of social theory depends. If human beings are just another entity, alongside plants, animals and things, what exactly are we and how do we differ from these other entities? What about consciousness, language, cognition and the ways in which we reproduce themselves socially and culturally? As Lucas (2012: 264) writes, 'archaeology is defined by its interest in the human'. If it had not been for humans, then there would be no cities, no state institutions, no social and economic classes, no styles of art and music, and no philosophies. To be fair, there are relational archaeologists who criticise symmetrical archaeology for its lack of concern with the study of people (Crellin 2020: 152) and argue that a flat ontology is 'a starting point' for study (Crellin 2020: 160–1).

Van Dyke (2021: 487) argues that concepts such as assemblages and networks are 'good to think with', but that humans are still central to our work as archaeologists.

> If we are only interested in charting relationships among entities, and we consider people no more important than any other entities in the network, then we have no logical means by which we can hold perpetrators of violence and suffering to be accountable for their actions...if our ontology is 'flat', what happens to inequalities and power relationships?
> (2021: 489)

How do such inequalities come about? What roles do the control of labour and production play in the development of such inequalities and human exploitation? In the same volume of *Cambridge Archaeological Journal*, McGuire (2021) defends the continuing relevance and strength of the relational approach of Marxism, and rejects the emphasis on posthumanism and flat ontologies within the current batch of relational archaeologies.

There is no doubt that the new relational approaches are striking out in different directions and that there is scope for debate between such different approaches, and between them as a whole and already existing theories. Given the durability of such theories, the history of pluralism within archaeological theory, and the internal politics (e.g. funding, institutions) of archaeology, it seems unlikely that existing social (and indeed biological) theories will disappear in the foreseeable future. One interesting question is this: how far will the new relational approaches lead to different ways of 'doing' archaeology?

HISTORY, TIME AND CHANGE?

The focus on change in human beings and their material worlds has been prevalent since the beginnings of archaeology. What kinds of change do we study (e.g. in cultures, social relations, gender relations), how long did such change take and how did it vary in time and space? Recent decades have seen the development of finer-scale chronologies of change through methods such as dendrochronology and Bayesian analysis of radiocarbon dating, allowing greater attention to be given to the timescale of individuals and social groupings in the past (e.g. Bayliss and Whittle 2015). But what about large-scale histories over centuries and millennia? How can we integrate histories at different scales? These are theoretical questions.

Archaeologists have revisited the study of change and issues of scale in recent years (e.g. Crellin 2020). Criticisms have been made of assumptions of 'timelessness' in the past of areas such as sub-Saharan Africa (MacEachern 2013) and the Mediterranean (Chapman 2014). Robb and Pauketat (2013a) criticise ahistorical approaches to change (e.g. structuralism, ANT – see Chapter 5), and the postprocessual focus on the local, individual human scale of analysis to the exclusion of 'big picture' histories. Instead, they propose a theoretical approach to 'the intersection of microscale human experience with histories as large-scale and long-term phenomena' (2013a: 3) that avoids some of the perceived defects in the work of the French Annales historian, Ferdnand Braudel, who distinguished different levels of time (individual, social and long-term), but did not give due theoretical attention to the linkages between them (2013a: 11–12). Key to these linkages is a relational approach to the study of historical processes that ties together longer-lasting cultural worlds, historical landscapes and cultural traditions and institutions, with shorter-lived histories and cycles of political and social development (2013a: 24–7). The interplay of these factors can lead to 'tipping points', that is rapid historical transformations. The range of case studies in Robb and Pauketat's (2013b) edited book will continue to be influential in debates on historical scales and change in the coming years.

EPISTEMOLOGY STILL MATTERS?

Although contemporary archaeological theory places prominent emphasis on ontology, issues of epistemology are still important. We may work with different theories, identify as different kinds of archaeologists, and work in different regional traditions and periods (e.g. prehistoric or historic archaeologies), but we all use archaeological evidence to produce knowledge of the past. Chapter 1 contains an introduction to how archaeologists have engaged with epistemological issues, especially in the debates between processual and postprocessual archaeologists in the 1970s and 1980s. Such debates centred on the utility, or otherwise, of idealised accounts of knowledge production drawn from different traditions of the philosophy of science. Chapman and Wylie (2016) argue that archaeology has gone quiet on such debates since the 1990s, leaving important questions unanswered. What gives us trust and confidence in our claims to knowledge of the cultural past? What can we learn from case studies about the ways in which archaeology works to produce knowledge? Chapman and Wylie (2016: 55–92) scrutinise fieldwork practices, how we bring new life to old evidence (93–141), how archaeology interacts as a 'trading zone' with 'external resources', such as radiocarbon dating and isotopic analyses (142–201) and revisit the concepts of truth and objectivity (203–16).

Drawing on the work of the philosopher Stephen Toulmin (1958), knowledge production is treated as a form of argument applicable to the ways in which practitioners in a particular 'domain' (in our case, archaeology) actually work and reason. A wide range of disciplines uses the metaphor of scaffolding to support the making of reliable observations and to put their data to work as evidence. In archaeology, this scaffolding ranges from finds' contexts (e.g. stratification, associations) through analytical techniques (e.g. methods of dating and provenance), to the strength or applicability of the theories we use, and the institutional structures that support archaeological practice). Such scaffolding can be useful, even if it is provisional. The knowledge we produce is always partial and evaluated for its trustworthiness rather than some abstract, all-or-nothing, concept of truth. Good examples of the varying success of such attempts at knowledge production include the Roman Diaspora (Box 1.5) and the use of lead-isotope analyses to study Bronze Age trade networks in the Mediterranean (Chapman and Wylie 2016: 164–84). More recently, Routledge (2021) has produced an informative and critical paper on the metaphor of scaffolding in the philosophy of science and in archaeology: among other observations, he notes how Childe used the metaphor to argue for the importance of the Three-Age system (Stone, Bronze and Iron Ages) in supporting understandings of relative chronology, change in technology and social evolution in the 1930s and 1940s. Routledge also stresses the provisional nature of any such scaffolding and the need for its regular re-examination.

Lucas (2019: 60–94, 199–20)) argues against the idea that there is just the one model (i.e. the Toulmin one) for the production of knowledge in archaeology, and presents a different model for what he calls 'a form of literary production', by which we 'translate things into words' (2019: 10). Is there a uniform structure and form of expression to archaeological texts, whether they be excavation reports, articles in professional periodicals, or monographs? Are our publications purely 'scientific' and 'learned', and not to be taken seriously if they are, for example, narratives, and thereby 'stories'? To answer such questions, Lucas (2019: 73–96) turns to examples of actual publications to examine which different types of expression and presentation (e.g. descriptive, narrative, argument) are used in relation to different forms of hard copy and online publications (e.g. books, journal articles, excavation monographs)? What specific values do these types have in the production of knowledge? Overall, his analysis is set within the context of examples of textual experimentation by archaeologists during the last two decades (2019: 70–3).

These are only partial accounts of such recent studies of knowledge production in archaeology and could be usefully supplemented by, for example, Orser (2015) and Gibbon (2014), but they are sufficient to illustrate how epistemology has come in from the cold since the turn of the millennium.

ISSUES OF POLITICS, IDENTITIES AND HERITAGE?

How do archaeologists work with scientists to produce knowledge about the past? This is by no means a new question, but it is central to the recent upsurge of archaeological, isotopic and ancient DNA analyses used to make inferences about kinship relations and population movements in the past. Critical evaluation of the challenges of such research and the reliability of the conclusions presented in both professional and popular publications has been raised, for example, by Frieman and Hofmann (2019). How far do archaeologists and scientists understand each other's assumptions, methods and ways of working? We have already seen how archaeological claims for total objectivity and political neutrality (see Chapter 1) are flawed. This is an important observation, as there is a danger that 'complex scientific data and equally complex social processes' (Frieman and Hofmann 2019: 532) may be simplified in such interdisciplinary research and in the dissemination of its results to heritage industries and popular audiences. There is an increasing demand for popular archaeologies (e.g. books, magazines, television programmes), driven by the expectations, interests and political agendas of the public (Hanscam 2021: 523; Hofmann and Frieman 2021: 520). Bonacchi *et al.* (2018) also show how archaeology and heritage studies can be used to shape political identities in the present. Their major, big data study of Facebook pages shows how decisions by predominantly UK-based users on whether to vote Leave or Remain in the UK Brexit Referendum of 2016 were shaped or supported by their knowledge of the past of Britain and Europe from the Iron Age to Medieval periods. For example, 'remainers' stressed the 'civilising power' of the Roman Empire (equated with the European Union), while 'leavers' regarded romanisation of Britain as a violent and oppressive process. Archaeology is always open to misuse, but this does not absolve archaeologists from the need for clarity and reflexivity about their work and the knowledge they produce. We have a responsibility to be vigilant and critical of simplified narratives of the past and how they are presented to the public.

Can biological approaches such as the analysis of ancient DNA lead us directly to reliable inferences about kinship, gender, ethnic and other forms of identity in the past? In other words, is social identity determined by biology? These questions are directly and provocatively addressed by Brück (2021), who criticises the inference of kinship relations (e.g. the monogamous nuclear family and descent through the male line) from a combination of isotopic, ancient DNA and archaeological research on the period between the Late Neolithic to the Early Bronze Age in Central Europe. Her central conclusions are twofold. First, 'kinship cannot be viewed as a direct reflection of genetic links. Kinship is not a given, or 'natural fact', but is a process, the outcome of culturally prescribed social practices that require careful nurture, work and commitment'. Second, we should 'avoid using genetic evidence in ways that unthinkingly impose modern conceptions of kinship and gender relations in the past' (2021: 235). These arguments will merit close examination and debate during the coming years.

THEORY AND PRACTICE?

Archaeological theory, like archaeology as a whole, is developed within, and constrained by, institutional contexts. The 'disciplinary alliances' (Jones 2009: 91–4) of archaeology, as seen within the structures of universities, include anthropology, history, ancient history, natural and environmental sciences, with consequences ranging from the contents of the syllabus through to access to resources (whether within individual universities or national or international funding bodies). Also critical is whether or not there is a critical mass of staff and researchers who can develop teaching in, and research on, existing or novel theoretical approaches. In some cases (e.g. agency, feminism and gender), it took at least a decade for major books, rather than individual articles, to be the subject of publication.

There are also still barriers to participation in theoretical debates (e.g. accessibility to publications, the challenges of translation of books and articles into English) for non-English speaking archaeologists outside the Anglo-American world. These challenges are not helped by the linguistic limitations of those for whom English is the native language. In the UK, access to the teaching of foreign languages has been declining in schools and universities since the end of the last millennium.

Further barriers can be seen in the varying degrees of institutional integration/separation of archaeological practice and theory between universities and full-time field-based organisations. In Chapter 1, we learned about the interrelationships between theory and practice in archaeology, but we also have to ask ourselves how far the reflexive archaeology with interpretation 'at the trowel's edge', as seen at the Turkish Neolithic site of Catalhoyuk, can be developed within the financial constraints under which most archaeological excavations are pursued? Archaeologists in the 2020s face a tough challenge in securing financial support, compared, for example, to the economic demands of climate change, the cost of the Covid-pandemic, and the increased military spending in Europe and North America as a consequence of the Ukraine-Russia war.

Cobb and Croucher (2014: 198) argue that teaching and learning (together known as pedagogy) of archaeology, as well as research on how, when and where we do this, are still topics that are fundamentally 'undervalued and therefore marginalised in archaeology in the UK and worldwide'. Factors contributing to this neglect include the lesser weight placed on teaching and learning, as opposed to research, by national and international funding bodies and universities deciding on promotions for individual academics (2014: 198–9). Teaching and research take place in both separate (e.g. classrooms, laboratories) and shared (e.g. excavations and surveys) contexts. The teaching of academic archaeologists is inspired and infused by their research topics (often trying out ideas and interpretations for future publications), while their fieldwork provides the context for involving student participation in this research. This breaks down the barrier between 'active' teachers and 'passive' students (e.g. Cobb and Croucher 2014: 8–12). Greater investment in pedagogy research in archaeology would support a closer interaction between teaching and learning, theory and practice.

'THE FIELD IS SO DIVERSE, GOING OFF IN ALL DIRECTIONS'

The themes, ideas and questions raised in this chapter by no means exhaust the potential for developments in archaeological theory in the next ten years. A cursory glance at the contents of recent issues of archaeological journals reveals that themes such as gender, landscapes, social memory, semiotics and meaning and identities are all still attracting attention and debate. Theoretical interests vary in popularity at all levels of archaeology, within and between university departments, and between different regions of the world. This variation is such that it defies any current attempt to make use of terms such as traditional, processual and postprocessual archaeologies as a valid representation of the diversity of contemporary theory and practice. This diversity inclines me to be sceptical about any claims that the future of archaeological theory during the 2020s can be subsumed within an overarching paradigm change with relational and non-relational approaches irrevocably and completely separated by a fault line. The archaeological world will be one of pluralism and diversity, productive debate, all shaped by the intellectual, political, institutional and economic contexts in which we live.

SUMMARY

- The history and development of archaeological theory suggest that, in this decade, there will still be competing theories, cycles of their popularity, intense debates within and between them, older and unfashionable theories will remain in circulation (however unpopular), and different theories will still be used to study shared problems of interest.
- The big questions concern how the new, relational archaeologies will develop and whether there will be more nuanced differences between them and non-relational, archaeological theories.
- Among themes of study, recent publications suggest further research on the theorising of change and the scales of such change, archaeological epistemology (especially how archaeologists and scientists work together to produce knowledge of the past), and how archaeological teaching, theory and practice are integrated. There will also be surprises.

- The institutional contexts and their funding, in which archaeology is taught and researched, will also shape the development of archaeological theory and practice.

FURTHER READING

Johnson (2020: 260–83) and Thomas (2015) provide personal glimpses into the future of archaeological theory that overlap, to a certain extent, with the views expressed in this chapter. The periodical *Cambridge Archaeological Review* (volume 31(3), 2021) contains an instructive, special section with papers on the merits and demerits of posthumanism in archaeology. Issues of time, history and change are discussed in Crellin (2020) and Robb and Pauketat (2013b). For those with a philosophical bent, Chapman and Wylie (2016) and Lucas (2019) disinter debates and developments on knowledge production in archaeology, while Orser (2015) discusses how archaeologists think and how this works to distinguish reliable archaeological knowledge from what can politely be called 'speculative conjectures'.

REFERENCES

Alcock, S. E. (1991) 'Tomb cult and the post-classical polis', *American Journal of Archaeology* 95: 447–67.

Alt, S. M. and Pauketat, T. R. (eds.) (2020) *New Materialisms, Ancient Urbanisms*, Abingdon: Routledge.

Althusser, L. (1972) *Politics and History*, London: NLB.

Andah, B. W. (1995) 'European encumbrances to the development of relevant theory in Africa', in P. J. Ucko (ed.) *Theory in Archaeology: A World Perspective*, 96–109, London: Routledge.

Atalay, S. (2008) 'Multivocality and indigenous archaeologies', in J. Habu, C. Fawcett and J. M. Matsunaga (eds.) *Evaluating Multiple Narratives*, 29–44, New York: Springer.

Atalay, S. (2012) *Community-Based Archaeology*, Berkeley: University of California Press.

Barker, P. (1977) *Techniques of Archaeological Excavation*, London: Batsford.

Bayliss, A. and Whittle, A. (2015) 'Uncertain on principle: combining lines of archaeological evidence to create chronologies', in R. Chapman and A. Wylie (eds.) *Material Evidence. Learning from Archaeological Practice*, 213–42, Abingdon: Routledge.

Belsey, C. (2002) *Poststructuralism. A Very Short Introduction*, Oxford: Oxford University Press.

Bender, B. (1978) 'Gatherer-hunter to farmer', *World Archaeology* 10(2): 204–22.

Bennett, J. (2010) *Vibrant Matter. A Political Ecology of Things*, London: Duke University Press.

Bentley, R. A., Lipo, C., Maschner, H. D.G. and Marler, B. (2008) 'Darwinian archaeologies', in R. A. Bentley, H. D. G. Maschner and C. Chippindale (eds.) *Handbook of Archaeological Theories*, 109–32, Lanham, MD: Altamira Press.

Berlin, I. (1978) *Karl Marx. His Life and Environment* (Fourth edition), Oxford: Oxford University Press.

Bernbeck, R. and McGuire, R. H. (2011a) 'A conceptual history of ideology and its place in archaeology', in R. Bernbeck and R. H. McGuire (eds.), *Ideologies in Archaeology*, 15–59, Tucson: University of Arizona Press.

Bernbeck, R. and McGuire, R. H. (eds.) (2011b) *Ideologies in Archaeology*, Tucson: University of Arizona Press.

Beteille, A. (2008) *Marxism & Class Analysis*, Oxford: Oxford University Press.

Binford, L. R. (1968) 'Archeological perspectives', in S. R. Binford and L. R. Binford (eds) *New Perspectives in Archeology*, 5–32, Chicago, IL: Aldine.

Binford, L. R. (1972) *An Archaeological Perspective*, New York: Academic Press.

Binford, L. R. (1977) 'General introduction', in L. R. Binford (ed.), *For Theory Building in Archaeology. Essays on Faunal Remains, Aquatic Resources, Spatial Analysis and Systematic Modelling*, 1–13, New York: Academic Press.

Binford, L. R. (1978) *Nunamiut Ethnoarchaeology*, New York: Academic Press.

Binford, L. R. (1981) *Bones. Ancient Men and Modern Myths*, New York: Academic Press.

Binford, L. R. (1982) 'Meaning, inference and the material record', in C. Renfrew and S. Shennan (eds) *Ranking, Resource and Exchange. Aspects of the Archaeology of Early European Society*, 160–3, Cambridge: Cambridge University Press.

Binford, S. R. and Binford, L. R. (eds) (1968) *New Perspectives in Archeology*, Chicago, IL: Aldine.

Bird, D. W. and O'Connell, J. F. (2006) 'Behavioral ecology and archaeology', *Journal of Archaeological Research* 14(2): 143–88.

Bird, D. W. and O'Connell, J. F. (2012) 'Human behavioral ecology', in I. Hodder (ed.) *Archaeological Theory Today* (Second edition), 37–61, Cambridge: Polity.

Blackledge, P. (2006) *Reflections on the Marxist Theory of History*, Manchester: Manchester University Press.

Blake, E. (2008) 'The Mycenaeans in Italy: a minimalist position', *Papers of the British School at Rome* 76: 1–34.

Bliege Bird, R. and Smith, E. A. (2005) 'Signaling theory, strategic interaction and symbolic capital', *Current Anthropology* 46(2): 221–48.

Bloch, M. (1985) *Marxism and Anthropology. The History of a Relationship*, Oxford: Oxford University Press.

Boivin, N. (2008) *Material Culture, Material Minds*, Cambridge: Cambridge University Press.

Bonacchi, C., Altaweel, M., and Krzyzanska, M. (2018) 'The heritage of Brexit: roles of the past in the construction of political identities through social media', *Journal of Social Archaeology* 18(2): 174–92.

Boozer, A. (2010) 'Memory and microhistory of an empire: domestic contexts in Roman Amheida, Egypt', in D. Boric (ed.) *Archaeology and Memory*, 138–57, Oxford: Oxbow Books.

Boric, D. (2010) 'Happy forgetting? Remembering and dismembering dead bodies at Vlasac', in D. Boric (ed.) *Archaeology and Memory*, 48–67, Oxford: Oxbow Books.

Bourdieu, P. (1970) 'The Berber house or the world reversed', *Social Science Information* 9: 151–70.

Bourdieu, P. (1977) *Outline of a Theory of Practice*, Cambridge: Cambridge University Press.

Boyd, R. and Richerson, P. J. (1985) *Culture and the Evolutionary Process*, Chicago, IL: University of Chicago Press.

Bradley, R. (1983) 'Archaeology, evolution and the public good: The intellectual development of General Pitt Rivers', *Archaeological Journal* 140: 1–9.

Bradley, R. (1993) *Altering the Earth,* Edinburgh: Society of Antiquaries of Scotland, Monograph Series Number 8.

Braidotti, R. (2013) *The Posthuman*, Cambridge: Polity.

Brittain, M. and Harris, O. J. T. (2010) 'Enchaining arguments and fragmenting assumptions: reconsidering the fragmentation debate in archaeology', *World Archaeology* 42: 581–94.

Broodbank, C. (2006) 'The origins of and early development of Mediterranean maritime activity', *Journal of Mediterranean Archaeology* 19(2): 199–230.

Brown, B. (2001) 'Thing theory', *Critical Inquiry* 28(1):1–22.

Bruchac, M. M., Hart, S. M. and Wobst, H. M.(eds.) (2010) *Indigenous Archaeologies. A Reader in Decolonization*, London: Routledge.

Brück, J. (2005) 'Experiencing the past? The development of a phenomenological archaeology in British prehistory', *Archaeological Dialogues* 12(1): 45–72.

Brück, J. (2021) 'Ancient DNA, kinship and relational identities in Bronze Age Britain', *Antiquity* 95: 228–37.

Brumfiel, E. M. (1991) 'Weaving and cooking: women's production in Aztec Mexico', in J. M. Gero and M. W. Conkey (eds.) *Engendering Prehistory. Women and Prehistory*, 224–51, Oxford: Blackwell.

Bryant, L., Smicek, N., and Harman, G. (eds.) (2011) *The Speculative Turn. Continental Materialism and Realism*, Melbourne: re. press.

Bunge, M. (2003) *Philsophical Dictionary*, Amherst, NY: Prometheus Books.

Buteux, V. and Jackson, R. (2000) 'Rethinking the 'rubbish pit in Medieval Winchester', in S. Roskams (ed.) *Interpreting Stratigraphy. Site Evaluation, Recording Procedures and Stratigraphic Analysis*, 193–6, Oxford: BAR International Series 910.

Butler, C. (2002) *Postmodernism. A Very Short Introduction*, Oxford: Oxford University Press.

Butler, J. (1990) *Gender Trouble. Feminism and the Subversion of Identity*, New York: Routledge.

Callinicos, A. (1976) *Althusser's Marxism*, London: Pluto Press.

Callinicos, A. (1983) *Marxism and Philosophy*, Oxford: Oxford University Press.

Callinicos, A. (1987) *Making History. Agency, Structure and Change in Social Theory*, Cambridge: Polity Press.

Callinicos. A. (1989) *Against Postmodernism. A Marxist Critique*, Cambridge: Polity Press.

Callinicos, A. (1991) *The Revenge of History. Marxism and the East European Revolutions*, Cambridge: Polity Press.

Callinicos, A. (1999) *The Revolutionary Ideas of Karl Marx* (Second edition), London: Bookmark Publications.

Callinicos, A. (2007) *Social Theory. A Historical Introduction* (Second edition), Cambridge: Polity Press.

Chang, H. (2012) *Is Water H$_2$O? Evidence, Realism and Pluralism*. Dordrecht: Springer.

Chapman, J. (1998) 'The impact of modern invasions and migrations on archaeological explanation. A biographical sketch of Marija Gimbutas', in M. Díaz-Andreu and M. L. Stig-Sørensen (eds) *Excavating Women. A History of Women in European Archaeology*, 295–314, London: Routledge.

Chapman, J. (2000) *Fragmentation in Archaeology. People, Places and Broken Objects in the Prehistory of South Eastern Europe*, London: Routledge.

Chapman, R. (2003) *Archaeologies of Complexity*, London: Routledge.

Chapman, R. (2008) 'Alternative States', in J. Habu, C. Fawcett and M. Matsunaga (eds.) *Evaluating Multiple Narratives: Beyond Nationalist, Colonialist, Imperialist Archaeologies*, 144–65, New York: Springer.

Chapman, R. (2014) 'Scales, interaction, and movement in later Mediterranean prehistory', in S. Souvatzi and A. Hadji (eds.) *Space and Time in Mediterranean Prehistory*, 32–48, Abingdon: Routledge.

Chapman, R. and Wylie, A. (2016) *Evidential Reasoning in Archaeology*, London: Bloomsbury.

Cherry, J. F. (1981) 'Pattern and process in the earliest colonisation of the Mediterranean islands', *Proceedings of the Prehistoric Society* 47: 41–68.

Cherry, J. F. (1990) 'The first colonization of the Mediterranean islands: a review of recent research', *Journal of Mediterranean Archaeology* 3(2): 145–221.

Childe, V. G. (1946) *Scotland before the Scots*, London: Methuen.

Childe, V. G. (1947) *History*, London: Cobbett Press.

Childe, V. G. (1956) *Society and Knowledge*, New York: Harper.

Clark, J. E. and Blake, M. (1994) 'The power of prestige: competitive generosity and the emergence of rank societies in lowland Mesoamerica', in E. Brumfiel and J. W. Fox (eds.) *Factional Competition and Political Development in the New World*, 17–30, Cambridge: Cambridge University Press.

Clark, J. G. D. (1952) *Prehistoric Europe. The Economic Basis,* London: Methuen.

Clarke, D. L. (1968) *Analytical Archaeology*, London: Methuen.

Clarke, D. L. (1972) 'A provisional model of an Iron Age society and its settlement system', in D. L. Clarke (ed.) *Models in Archaeology*, 801–70, London: Methuen.

Clarke, D. L. (1973) 'Archaeology: the loss of innocence', *Antiquity* 47: 6–18.

Clarke, D. L. (1976) 'Mesolithic Europe: the economic basis', in G. de G. Sieveking, I. H. Longworth and K. E. Wilson (eds.) *Problems in Economic and Social Archaeology*, 449–81, London: Duckworth.

Clarke, G. (1979) *Pre-Roman and Roman Winchester, Part 2: The Roman Cemetery at Lankhills*, Oxford: Clarendon Press.

Cobb, H. and Croucher, K. (2014) 'Assembling archaeological pedagogy. A theoretical framework for valuing pedagogy in archaeological interpretation and practice', *Archaeological Dialogues* 21(2): 197–216.

Colebrook, C. (2002) *Gilles Deleuze*, London: Routledge.

Collingwood, R. G. (1939) *An Autobiography*, Oxford: Oxford University Press.

Colwell-Chanthaphonh, C. (2012) 'Archaeology and indigenous collaboration', in I. Hodder (ed.) *Archaeological Theory Today*. Second edition, 267–91, Cambridge: Polity.

Conkey, M. W. and Spector, J. (1984) 'Archaeology and the study of gender', *Archaeological Method and Theory* 7: 1–38.

Connerton, P. (1989) *How Societies Remember*, Cambridge: Cambridge University Press.

Connolly, J. (2017) 'Costly signalling in archaeology: origins, relevance, challenges and prospects', *World Archaeology* 49(4): 35–45.

Crellin, R. J. (2020) *Change and Archaeology*, London: Routledge.

Crellin, R. J., Cipolla, C. N., Montgomery L. M., Harris, O. J. T. and Moore, S. V. (2021) *Archaeological Theory in Dialogue*, London: Routledge.

Croucher, K. (2005) 'Queerying Near Eastern archaeology', *World Archaeology* 37(4): 610–20.

Darwin, C. (1859) *On the Origin of Species by Means of Natural Selection: of the Preservation of Favoured Races in the Struggle for Life*, London: Dent.

Darwin, C. (1871) *The Descent of Man and Selection in Relation to Sex*, London: John Murray.

Deetz, J. (1968) 'The inference of residence and descent rules from archaeological data', in S. R. Binford and L. R. Binford (eds), *New Perspectives in Archeology*, 41–9, Chicago, IL: Aldine.

Deetz, J. (1996) *In Small Things Forgotten. An Archaeology of Early American Life*, New York: Anchor Books.

DeLanda, M. (2016) *Assemblage Theory*, Edinburgh: Edinburgh Press.

Deleuze, G. and Guattari, F. (1987) *A Thousand Plateaus*, London: Bloomsbury.

Delgado Raack, S and Risch, R. (2008) 'Lithic perspectives on metallurgy: an example from Copper and Bronze Age South-East Iberia', in L. Longo and N. Skakun (eds.) *"Prehistoric Technology" 40 Years Later: Functional Studies and the Russian Legacy*, 235–51, Oxford: BAR International Series 1783.

Der, L. and Fernandini, F. (eds.) (2016) *Archaeology of Entanglement*, Abingdon: Routledge.

Derber, C. (2011) *Marx's Ghost. Midnight Conversations on Changing the World*, Boulder, CO: Paradigm Publishers.

Desmond, A. and Moore, J. (1991) *Darwin*, New York: Warner Books Inc.

De Vries, G. (2016) *Bruno Latour*, Cambridge: Polity.

Díaz-Andreu, M. and Lucy, S. (eds.) (2005) *Archaeology of Identity*, London: Routledge.

Díaz-Guardamino, M., Sanjuán, G. and Wheatley, D. (eds.) (2015) *The Lives of Prehistoric Monuments in Iron Age, Roman and Medieval Europe*, Oxford: Oxford University Press.

Dobres, M-A and Robb, J. (eds.) (2000) *Agency in Archaeology*, London: Routledge.

Dornan, J. L. (2002) 'Agency and archaeology: past, present and future directions', *Journal of Archaeological Method and Theory* 9(4): 303–29.

Dowson, T. (2000) 'Why queer archaeology? An introduction', *World Archaeology* 32(2): 161–5.

Dunbar, R., Barrett, L. and Lycett, J. (2007) *Evolutionary Psychology*, London: Oneworld Publications

Dunnell, R. C. (1978) 'Style and function: a fundamental dichotomy', *American Antiquity* 43: 192–202.

Eagleton, T. (2011) *Why Marx Was Right*, New Haven, CT and London: Yale University Press.

Earle, T. and Spriggs, M. (2015) 'Political economy in prehistory. A Marxist Approach to Pacific sequences', *Current Anthropology* 56(3): 515–44.

Eckardt, H., Chenery, C., Booth, P., Evans, J., Lamb, A. and Müldner, G. (2009) 'Oxygen and strontium isotope evidence for mobility in Roman Winchester', *Journal of Archaeological Science* 36: 2816–25.

Eckardt, H., Müldner, G. and Lewis, M. (2014) 'People on the move in Roman Britain', *World Archaeology* 46(4): 534–50.

Edgeworth, M. (2012) 'Follow the cut, follow the rhythm, follow the material', *Norwegian Archaeological Review* 45(1): 76–92.

Eerkens, J. W. and Lipo, C. P. (2005) 'Cultural transmission, copying errors, and the generation of variation in material culture and the archaeological record', *Journal of Anthropological Archaeology* 24: 316–34.

Ellen, R. (1982) *Environment, Subsistence and System. The Ecology of Small-scale Social Formations*, Cambridge: Cambridge University Press.

Engels, F. (1972) *The Origin of the Family, Private Property and the State*, New York: Pathfinder.

Faulkner, N. (2001) *The Decline and Fall of Roman Britain*, Stroud: Tempus.

Flannery, K. V. (1968) 'Archaeological systems theory and early Mesoamerica'. In B. J. Meggers (ed.) *Anthropological Archaeology in the Americas*, 67–87, Washington, DC: Anthropological Society of Washington.

Flannery, K. V. (1973) 'Archaeology with a capital S', in C. L. Redman (ed.), *Research and Theory in Current Archaeology*, 47–58, New York: Wiley.

Foot, P. (2012) *The Vote. How It Was Won and How It Was Undermined*, London: Bookmarks.

Fowler, C. (2004) *The Archaeology of Personhood*, Abingdon: Routledge.

Fox, C. (1932) *The Archaeology of the Cambridge Region*, Cambridge: Cambridge University Press.

Frankenstein, S. and Rowlands, M. (1978) 'The internal structure and regional context of Early Iron Age society in south-western Germany', *Bulletin of the Institute of Archaeology London* 15: 73–112.

Fried, M. H. (1967) *The Evolution of Political Society*, New York: Random House.

Friedman, J. (1974) 'Marxism, structuralism and vulgar materialism', *Man* 9: 444–69.

Friedman, J. and Rowlands, M. J. (1978) 'Notes towards an epigenetic model of the evolution of "civilisation"', in J. Friedman and M. J. Rowlands (eds.) *The Evolution of Social Systems*, 201–76, London: Duckworth.

Frieman, C. J. and Hofmann, D. (2019) 'Present pasts in the archaeology of genetics, identity, and migration in Europe: a critical essay', *World Archaeology* 51: 528–45.

Fromm, E. (1969) *Marx's Concept of Man*, New York: Frederick Ungar.

Galle, J. E. (2010) 'Costly signaling and gendered social strategies among slaves in the eighteenth-century Chesapeake: an archaeological perspective', *American Antiquity* 75(1): 19–43.

Gamble, C. (2015) *Archaeology. The Basics* (Third edition), Abingdon: Routledge.

Gamble, C., Gowlett, J. and Dunbar, R. (2014) *Thinking Big. How the Evolution of Social Life Shaped the Human Mind,* London: Thames and Hudson.

Geras, N. (1983) *Marx and Human Nature. Refutation of a Legend*, London: Verso.

Gero, J. M. (1991) 'Genderlithics: women's roles in stone tool production', in J. M. Gero and M. W. Conkey (eds) *Engendering Archaeology. Women and Prehistory*, 163–93, Oxford: Blackwell.

Gero, J. M. and Conkey, M. W. (eds.) (1991) *Engendering Archaeology. Women and Prehistory*, Oxford: Blackwell.

Gibbon, G. (2014) *Critically Reading the Theory and Methods of Archaeology. An Introductory Guide*, Lanham, MD: Altamira Press.

Giddens, A. (1984) *The Constitution of Society: Outline of the Theory of Structuration*, Cambridge: Polity Press.

Gilchrist, R. (1999) *Gender and Archaeology*, London: Routledge.

Gosden, C. (1985) 'Gifts and kin in Early Iron Age Europe', *Man* 20: 475–93.

Gosden, C. (1992) 'Endemic doubt: is what we write right?', *Antiquity* 66: 803–8.

Gosden, C. (1994) *Social Being and Time*, Oxford: Blackwell.

Gosden, C. (1999) *Anthropology and Archaeology*, London: Routledge.

Gosden, C. (2012) 'Post-colonial archaeology', in I. Hodder (ed.) *Archaeological Theory Today*. Second edition, 251–66, Cambridge: Polity.

Gosden, C. and Marshall, Y. (1999) 'The cultural biography of objects', *World Archaeology* 31: 169–78.

Green, S. (1981) *Prehistorian. A Biography of V. Gordon Childe*, Bradford-on-Avon: Moonraker.

Hadji and Souvatzi. (2014) *Space and Time in Mediterranean Prehistory*, Abingdon: Routledge.

Hamilakis, Y. (1998) 'Eating the dead: mortuary feasting and the politics of memory in the Aegean Bronze Age societies', in K. Branigan (ed.) *Cemetery and Society in the Aegean Bronze Age*, 115–32, Sheffield: Sheffield Academic Press.

Hamilakis, Y. (2013) *Archaeology of the Senses. Human Experience, Memory and Affect*, Cambridge: Cambridge University Press.

Hands, G. (2015) *Marx. A Complete Introduction*, London: Hodder & Stoughton.

Hanscam, E. (2021) 'The postnational critique – a response to reactionary populism?', *European Journal of Archaeology* 24(4): 523–26.

Harman, G. (2010) Technology, objects and things in Heidegger', *Cambridge Journal of Economics* 34: 17–25.

Harraway, D. (2003) *The Companion Species Manifesto: Dogs, People and Significant Otherness*, Chicago, IL: Chicago University Press.

Harris, O. J. T. (2013) 'Relational communities in Neolithic Britain', in C. Watts (ed.) *Relational Archaeologies: Humans, Animals, Things*, 173–89, Abingdon: Routledge.

Harris. O. J. T. (2018) 'More than representation: multiscalar assemblages and the Deleuzian challenge to Archaeology', *History of the Human Sciences* 31(3): 83–104.

Harris, O. J. T. and Cipolla, C. N. (2017) *Archaeological Theory in the New Millennium. Introducing Current Perspectives*, Abingdon: Routledge.

Harvey, D. (2010) *A Companion to Marx's Capital*, London: Verso.

Hastorf, C. (2003) 'Community with the ancestors: ceremonies and social memory in the Middle Formative at Chiripa, Bolivia', *Journal of Anthropological Archaeology* 22(4): 305–32.

Hawkes, C. F. C. (1954) 'Archaeological theory and method: some suggestions from the Old World', *American Anthropologist* 56: 155–68.

Hayden, B. (1995) 'Pathways to power. Principles for creating socioeconomic inequalities', in T. D. Price and G. M. Feinman (eds.) *Foundations of Social Inequality*, 15–86, New York: Plenum.

Hayden, B. (2014) *The Power of Feasts. From Prehistory to the Present*, Cambridge: Cambridge University Press.

Hays-Gilpin, K. and Wheatley, D. S. (eds.) (1998) *Reader in Gender Archaeology*, London: Routledge.

Hegmon, M. (2003) 'Setting theoretical egos aside: issues and theory in North American archaeology', *American Antiquity* 68: 213–43.

Hegmon, M., Howard, J. B., O'Hara, M. and Peeples, M. A. (2016) 'Path dependence and the long-term trajectory of prehistoric Hohokam irrigation in Arizona', in L. Der and F. Fernandini (eds.) *Archaeology of Entanglement*, 173–88, Abingdon: Routledge.

Heidegger, M. (1962) *Being and Time*, Oxford: Blackwell.

Hempel, C. G. (1966) *Philosophy of Natural Science*, Princeton, NJ: Prentice-Hall.

Hobsbawm, E. (2011) *How to Change the World. Marx and Marxism 1840–2011*, London: Little, Brown.

Hodder, I. (ed.) (1978) *The Spatial Organisation of Culture*, London: Duckworth.

Hodder, I. (1982a) *Symbols in Action. Ethnoarchaeological Studies of Material Culture*, Cambridge: Cambridge University Press.

Hodder, I. (ed.) (1982b) *Symbolic and Structural Archaeology*, Cambridge: Cambridge University Press.

Hodder, I. (ed.) (1982c) 'The identification and interpretation of ranking in prehistory: a contextual perspective', in C. Renfrew and S. Shennan (eds) *Ranking, Resource and Exchange. Aspects of the Archaeology of Early European Society*, 150–4, Cambridge: Cambridge University Press.

Hodder, I. (1986) *Reading the Past. An Introduction to Anthropology for Archaeologists*, London: Batsford.

Hodder, I. (ed.) (1987) *Archaeology as Long-Term History*, Cambridge: Cambridge University Press.

Hodder, I. (1988) 'Material culture texts and social change: a theoretical discussion and some archaeological examples', *Proceedings of the Prehistoric Society* 54: 67–75.

Hodder, I. (1989) 'Comments on Archaeology into the 1990s', *Norwegian Archaeological Review* 22(1): 15–18.

Hodder, I. (1997) 'Always momentary, fluid and flexible: towards a reflexive excavation methodology', *Antiquity* 71: 691–700.

Hodder, I. (1999) *The Archaeological Process. An Introduction*, Blackwell: Oxford.

Hodder, I. (2000) 'Agency and individuals in long-term processes', in M-A. Dobres and J. Robb (eds.) *Agency in Archaeology*, 21–33, London: Routledge.

Hodder, I. (ed.) (2012a) *Archaeological Theory Today* (Second edition), Cambridge: Polity Press.

Hodder, I. (ed.) (2012b) 'Introduction. Contemporary theoretical debate in archaeology', in I. Hodder (ed.) *Archaeological Theory Today*. Second edition, 1–14, Cambridge: Cambridge University Press.

Hodder, I. (2012c) *Entangled. An Archaeology of the Relationships between Humans and Things*, Oxford: Wiley-Blackwell.

Hodder, I. (2016) *Studies in Human-Thing Entanglement*, http://www.ian-hodder.com/books/studies-human-thing- entanglement. Accessed 1 September 2021.

Hodder, I. (2018) *Where Are We Heading? The Evolution of Humans and Things*, New Haven, CT and London: Templeton.

Hodder, I. (2019) 'Contested history-making as part of the building of social networks at Neolithic Catalhoyuk, Turkey, in S. Souvatzi, A. Baysal and E. L. Baysal (eds.) *Time and History in Prehistory*, 250–62, Abingdon: Routledge.

Hodder, I. and Hutson, S. (2003) *Reading the Past. Current Approaches to Interpretation in Archaeology* (Third edition), Cambridge: Cambridge University Press.

Hofmann, D. and Frieman, C. J. (2021) 'Introduction: archaeology and populism', *European Journal of Archaeology* 2024(4): 519–23.

Hosfield, R. (2009) 'Modes of transmission and material culture patterns in craft skills', in S. Shennan (ed.) *Pattern and Process in Cultural Evolution*, 45–60, Berkeley: University of California Press.

Humle, T. (2010) 'Material culture in primates', in D. Hicks and M.C. Beaudry (eds.) *The Oxford Handbook of Material Culture Studies*, 406–24, Oxford: Oxford University Press.

Hunt, R. C. and Gilman, A. (eds.) (1998) *Property in Economic Context*, Lanham, MD: University Press of America.

Hunt, T. (2009) *The Frock-Coated Communist. The Revolutionary Life of Friedrich Engels*, London: Allen Lane.

Inglis, D. and Thorpe, C. (2019) *An Invitation to Social Theory* (Second edition), Cambridge: Polity Press.

Ingold, T. (1993) 'The temporality of landscape', *World Archaeology* 25(2): 152–74.

Ingold, T. (1996) 'Hunting and gathering as ways of perceiving the environment', in R. Ellen and K. Fukui (eds.) *Redefining Nature, Ecology, Culture and Domestication*, 117–55, Oxford: Berg.

Ingold, T. (2000) *The Perception of the Environment*, London: Routledge.

Ingold, T. (2007) 'Materials against materiality', *Archaeological Dialogues* 14: 1–16.

Ingold, T. (2011) *Being Alive. Essays on Movement, Knowledge and Description*, Abingdon: Routledge.

Ingold, T. (2013) *Making*, Abingdon: Routledge.

Ingold, T. (2018) *Anthropology. Why it Matters, Cambridge*: Polity Press.

Inwood, M. (2019) *Heidegger. A Very Short Introduction*, Oxford: Oxford University Press.

Jervis, B. (2016) 'Assemblage theory and town foundation in medieval England', *Cambridge Archaeological Journal* 26(3): 381–95.

Jervis, B. (2019) *Assemblage Thought in Archaeology*, Abingdon: Routledge.

Jochim, M. A. (1976) *Hunter-Gatherer Subsistence and Settlement. A Predictive Model*, New York: Academic Press.

Jochim, M. A. (1981) *Strategies for Survival. Cultural Behavior in an Ecological Context*, New York: Academic Press.

Johnson, M. (1989) 'Conceptions of agency in archaeological interpretation', *Journal of Anthropological Archaeology* 8: 189–211.

Johnson, M. (2020) *Archaeological Theory. An Introduction*, London: Wiley-Blackwell.

Jones, A. (2002) *Archaeological Theory and Scientific Practice*, Cambridge: Cambridge University Press.

Jones, A. (2004) 'Archaeometry and materiality: materials-based analysis in theory and practice', *Archaeometry* 46: 327–38.

Jones, A. (2005) 'Lives in fragments? Personhood in the European Neolithic', *Journal of Social Archaeology* 5: 193–224.

Jones, A. (2009) 'Into the future', in B. Cunliffe, C. Gosden and R. A. Joyce (eds.) *The Oxford Handbook of Archaeology*, 89–114, Oxford: Oxford University Press.

Jones, A. (2012) *Prehistoric Materialities. Becoming Material in Britain and Ireland*, Oxford: Oxford University Press.

Jones, M. (2005) 'Ecological archaeology', in C. Renfrew and P. Bahn (eds.) *Archaeology. The Key Concepts*, 79–84, Abingdon: Routledge.

Jones, S. (1997) *The Archaeology of Identity. Constructing Identities in the Past and Present*, London: Routledge.

Jones, S. (2006) *Antonio Gramsci*, London: Routledge.

Keegan, W. F. and J. M. Diamond (1987) 'Colonization of islands by humans: a biogeographical perspective', *Advances in Archaeological Method and Theory* 10: 49–92.

Kirch, P.V. and Green, R. (1987) 'History, phylogeny and evolution in Polynesia', *Current Anthropology* 28: 431–56.

Knapp, A. B. (1996) 'Archaeology without gravity: postmodernism and the past', *Journal of Archaeological Method and Theory* 3(2): 127–58.

Knappett, C. (2011) *An Archaeology of Interaction. Network Perspectives on Material Culture & Society*, Oxford: Oxford University Press.

Knappett, C. (2012) 'Materiality', in I. Hodder (ed.) *Archaeological Theory Today*. Second edition, 188–207, Cambridge: Polity Press.

Kohler, T. A. (2012) 'Complex systems and archaeology, in I. Hodder (ed.) *Archaeological Theory Today*. Second edition, 91–123, Cambridge: Polity Press.

Krader, L. (1972) *The Ethnological Notebooks of Karl Marx*, Assen:Van Gorcum & Comp.

Kristiansen, K. (1998) *Europe before History*, Cambridge: Cambridge University Press.

Kristiansen, K. (2004) 'Genes versus agents: a discussion of the widening theoretical gap in archaeology', *Archaeological Dialogues* 11(2): 77–99.

Kristiansen, K. (2009) 'The discipline of archaeology', in B. Cunliffe, C. Gosden and R. A. Joyce (eds.) *The Oxford Handbook of Archaeology*, 3–46, Oxford: Oxford University Press.

Kuijt, I. (2008) 'The regeneration of life. Neolithic structures of symbolic remembering and forgetting', *Current Anthropology* 49(2): 171–97.

Latour, B. (1987) *Science in Action*, Milton Keynes: Open University Press.

Latour, B. (2005) *Reassembling the Social: An Introduction to Actor-Network-Theory*, Oxford: Oxford University Press.

Layton, R. (1997) *An Introduction to Theory in Anthropology*, Cambridge: Cambridge University Press.

Leacock, E. (1983) 'Interpreting the origins of gender inequality: conceptual and historical problems', *Dialectical Anthropology* 7: 263–84.

Lechte, J. (1994) *Fifty Key Contemporary Thinkers. From Structuralism to Postmodernity*, London: Routledge.

Lenin, V. I. (1917) *The State and Revolution*, London: Central Books.

Leone, M. P., Parker, B., Potter Jr, and Shackel, P. A. (1987) 'Towards a critical archaeology', *Current Archaeology* 28: 283–302.

Leppard, T. P. and Fitzpatrick, S. M. (2021) 'Theory beyond the calm ocean? The Pacific contribution to global island archaeology', in T. Thomas (ed.) *Theory in the Pacific, the Pacific in Theory. Archaeological Perspectives*, 37–57, Abingdon: Routledge.

Levi- Strauss, C. (1963) *Structural Anthropology*, New York: Basic Books.

Lucas, G. (2012) *Understanding the Archaeological Record*, Cambridge: Cambridge University Press.

Lucas, G. (2015) 'The mobility of theory', *Current Swedish Archaeology* 23: 13–32.

Lucas, G. (2016) 'The paradigm concept in archaeology', *World Archaeology* 49(2): 260–70.

Lucas, G. (2019) *Writing the Past. Knowledge and Literary Production in Archaeology*, Abingdon: Routledge.

Lukács, G. (1923) *History and Class Consciousness*, London: Merlin.

Lull, V. and Micó, R. (2011) *Archaeology and the Origin of the State. The Theories*, Oxford: Oxford University Press.

Lull, V., Micó, R., Rihuete, C. and Risch, R. (2005) 'Property relations in the Bronze Age of South-western Europe: an archaeological analysis of infant burials from El Argar (Almería, Spain)', *Proceedings of the Prehistoric Society* 71: 247–68.

Lycett, S. J. and Shennan, S. (2018) 'David Clarke's *Analytical Archaeology* at 50', *World Archaeology* 50: 210–20.

MacArthur, R. H. and Wilson, E. O. (1967) *The Theory of Island Biogeography*, Princeton, NJ: Princeton University Press.

MacEachern, S. (2013) 'Time on the timeless continent: history and archaeological chronologies in the southern Lake Chad Basin', in J. Robb and T. R. Pauketat (eds.) (2013b) *Big Histories, Human Lives. Tackling Problems of Scale in Archaeology*, 123–44, Santa Fe: School For Advanced Research Press.

Mann. M. (1986) *The Sources of Social Power*, Vol 1. Cambridge: Cambridge University Press.

Marks, J. (2009) The nature of humanness, in B. Cunliffe, C. Gosden and R. A. Joyce (eds.) *The Oxford Handbook of Archaeology*, 237–53, Oxford: Oxford University Press.

Marx, K. (1964) *Pre-capitalist Economic Formations*, New York: International Publishers.

Marx, K. (1969) 'Economic and philosophical manuscripts', in E. Fromm (ed.) *Marx's Concept of Man*, 85–196, New York: Frederick Ungar.

Marx, K. (1972) *Capital*. Vol 1, London: J. M. Dent and Sons Ltd.

Marx, K. (1973) *Grundrisse. Foundations of the Critique of Political Economy (Rough Draft)*, London: Penguin Books.

Marx, K. (2010) *The 18th Brumaire of Louis Bonaparte*, New York: International Publishers.

Marx, K. and Engels, F. (1970) *The German Ideology. Part One*, London: Lawrence & Wishart.

Marx, K. and Engels, F. (1998) *The Communist Manifesto. A Modern Edition* (Edited by E. Hobsbawm), London: Verso.

Matthews, C. N., Leone, M. P. and Jordan, K. A. (2002) 'The political economy of archaeological cultures', *Journal of Social Archaeology* 2(1):109–34.

McClellan, D. (1998) *Marxism after Marx*, London: Macmillan Press.

McGuire, K. R. and Hildebrandt, W. R. (2005) 'Rethinking Great Basin foragers: prestige hunting and costly signaling during the Middle Archaic period', *American Antiquity* 70(4): 695–712.

McGuire, R. H. (1988) 'Dialogues with the dead. Ideology and the cemetery', in M. P. Leone and P. B. Potter Jr (eds.) *The Recovery of Meaning. Historical Archaeology in the Eastern United States*, 435–80, Washington, DC: Smithsonian Institution Press.

McGuire, R. H. (1989) 'The greater Southwest as a periphery of Mesoamerica,' in T. C. Champion (ed.) *Centre and Periphery: Comparative Studies in Archaeology*, 40–66, London: Routledge.

McGuire, R. H. (2002) *A Marxist Archaeology* (Second edition), New York: Percheron Press.

McGuire, R. H. (2008) *Archaeology as Political Action*, Berkeley: University of California Press.

McGuire, R. H. (2021) 'A relational Marxist critique of posthumanism in archaeology', *Cambridge Archaeological Journal* 31(3): 495–501.

McGuire, R. H., O'Donovan and Wurst, L. (2005) 'Probing praxis in archaeology: the last eighty years', *Rethinking Marxism* 17: 355–72.

McLellan, D. (1998) *Marxism After Marx* (Third edition), London: Macmillan Press.

McNairn, B. (1980) *The Method and Theory of V. Gordon Childe*, Edinburgh: Edinburgh University Press.

Merleau-Ponty, M. (1962) *Phenomenology of Perception*, London: Routledge.

Meskell, L. (1999) *Archaeologies of Social Life*, Oxford: Blackwell.

Meskell, L. (2002) 'The intersections of identity and politics in archaeology', *Annual Review of Anthropology* 31: 279–301.

Metcalf, P. (2005) *Anthropology. The Basics*, Abingdon: Routledge.

Miller, D. and Tilley, C. (eds.) (1984) *Ideology, Power and Prehistory*, Cambridge: Cambridge University Press.

Mithen, S. (1998) *The Prehistory of Mind. A Search for the Origins of Art, Religion and Science*, London: Phoenix.

Mithen, S. (2001) 'Archaeological theory and theories of cognitive evolution', in I. Hodder (ed.) *Archaeological Theory Today*, 98–121, Cambridge: Polity Press.

Moffett, A. J. and Chirikure, S. (2016) 'Exotica in context: reconfiguring prestige, power and wealth in the Southern African Iron Age', *Journal of World Prehistory* 29: 337–82.

Montgomery, L. (2021) 'Indigenous alterity as archaeological praxis', in R. Crellin *et al.* (eds.) *Archaeological Theory in Dialogues*, 51–68, Abingdon: Routledge.

Morgan, L. H. (1877) *Ancient Society*, New York: Holt.

Muller, J. (1997) *Mississippian Political Economy*, New York: Plenum Press.

Nagaoka, L. (2002) 'The effects of resource depression on foraging efficiency, diet breadth, and patch use in southern New Zealand', *Journal of Anthropological Archaeology* 21(4): 419–42.

Nicholas, G. and Markey, N. (2015) 'Traditional knowledge, archaeological evidence, and other ways of knowing', in R. Chapman and A. Wylie (eds.) *Material Evidence. Learning from Archaeological Practice*, 287–307, Abingdon: Routledge.

Olsen, B. (2010) *In Defense of Things. Archaeology and the Ontology of Objects*, Lanham, MD: Altamira Press.

Olsen, B. (2012) 'Symmetrical archaeology', in I. Hodder (ed.) *Archaeological Theory Today*. Second edition, 208–28, Cambridge: Polity.

Olsen, B., Shanks, M., Webmoor, T. and Witmore, C. (2012) *Archaeology. The Discipline of Things*, Berkeley: University of California Press.

Orser, C. H. (2015) *Archaeological Thinking. How to Make Sense of the Past*, Lanham, MD: Rowman and Littlefield.

Parker Pearson, M. (1996) 'Food fertility and front doors: houses in the first millennium', in T. Champion and J. R. Collis (eds.) *The Iron Age in Britain and Ireland: Recent Trends*, 117–32, Sheffield: Sheffield Academic Press.

Parkinson, W. A. (ed.) (2002) *The Archaeology of Tribal Societies*, Ann Arbor: International Monographs in Prehistory.

Parkinson, W. A. and Galaty, M. L. (eds.) (2009) *Ancient State Interaction: The Eastern Mediterranean in the Bronze Age*, Santa Fe: School for Advanced Research Press.

Patterson, T. C. (2003) *Marx's Ghost. Conversations with Archaeologists*, Oxford: Berg.

Patterson, T. C. (2009) *Karl Marx, Anthropologist*, Oxford: Berg.

Pauketat, T. R. (2000) 'The tragedy of the commoners', in M-E Dobres and J. Robb (eds.) *Agency in Archaeology*, 112–29, London: Routledge.

Paynter, R. and McGuire, R. H. (1991) 'The archaeology of inequality: material culture, domination, and resistance', in R. Paynter and R. H. McGuire (eds.) *The Archaeology of Inequality*, 1–24, Oxford: Blackwell.

Pierce, E., Russell, A., Maldonado, A. and Cambell, L. (eds.) (2016) *Creating Material Worlds: The Use of Identity in Archaeology*, Oxford: Oxbow Books.

Pluciennik, M. (2005) *Social Evolution*, London: Duckworth.

Pluciennik, M. (2011) 'Theory, fashion, culture', in J. Bintliff and Mark Pearce (eds.) *The Death of Archaeological Theory*, 31–47, Oxford: Oxbow Books.

Pollard, J. (2004) 'The art of decay and the transformation of substance', in C. Renfrew, C. Gosden and E. DeMarrais (eds.) *Substance, Memory, Display*, 47–62, Cambridge: McDonald Institute for Archaeological Research.

Praetzellis, A. (2015) *Archaeological Theory in a Nutshell*, Walnut Creek, CA: Left Coast Press.

Prentiss, A. M. (2021) 'Theoretical plurality, the extended evolutionary synthesis, and archaeology', *Proceedings of the National Academy of Sciences of the United States of America* 118(2): 1–9.

Preucel, R. W. (2006) *Archaeological Semiotics*, Oxford: Blackwells.

Preucel, R. W. and Hodder, I. (eds.) (1996) *Contemporary Archaeology in Theory*, Oxford: Blackwell Publishers Ltd.

Preucel, R. W. and Mrozowski, S. A. (eds.) (2010) *Contemporary Archaeology in Theory. The New Pragmatism*, Oxford: Wiley-Blackwell.

Price, T. D. (1995) 'Social inequality at the origins of agriculture', in T. D. Price and G. M. Feinman (eds.) *Foundations of Social Complexity*, 129–51, New York: Plenum Press.

Raab, L. M. and Goodyear, A. C. (1984) 'Middle-range theory in archaeology: a critical review of origins and applications', *American Antiquity* 49: 255–68.

Rathje, W. L., Shanks, M. and Witmore, C. (eds.) (2013) *Archaeology in the Making. Conversation through a Discipline*, Abingdon: Routledge.

Rees, J. (1994) 'Engels' Marxism', in J. Rees (ed.) *The Revolutionary Ideas of Frederick Engels*, 47–82, International Socialism 65, Special Issue.

Renfrew, C. (1973) 'Monuments, mobilisation and social organisation in Neolithic Wessex', in C. Renfrew (ed.) *The Explanation of Cultural Change: Models in Prehistory*, 539–58, London: Duckworth.

Renfrew, C. (1994) 'Towards a cognitive archaeology', in C. Renfrew and E. B. W. Zubrow (eds.) *The Ancient Mind. Elements of Cognitive Archaeology*, 3–12, Cambridge: Cambridge University Press.

Renfrew, C. (2012) 'Towards a cognitive archaeology. Material engagement and the early development of society', in I. Hodder (ed.) *Archaeological Theory Today*. Second edition, 124–45, Cambridge: Polity Press.

Renfrew, C. and Bahn, P. (eds.) (2005) *Archaeology. The Key Concepts*, London: Routledge.

Renfrew, C. and Bahn, P. (eds.) (2012) *Archaeology. Theories, Methods and Practice*, London: Thames and Hudson.

Renfrew, C. and Zubrow, E. B. W. (eds.) (1994) *The Ancient Mind. Elements of Cognitive Archaeology*, Cambridge: Cambridge University Press.

Rigby, S. H. (1992) *Engels and the Formation of Marxism. History, Dialectics and Evolution*, Manchester: Manchester University Press.

Risch, R. (2008) 'From production traces to social organisation: towards an epistemology of functional analysis', in L. Longo and N. Skakun (eds.) *"Prehistoric Technology" 40 Years Later: Functional Studies and the Russian Legacy*, 513–21, Oxford: BAR International Series 1783.

Robb, J. and Harris, O. J. T. (eds.) (2013) *The Body in History. Europe from the Palaeolithic to the Future*, Cambridge: Cambridge University Press.

Robb, J. and Pauketat, T. R. (2013a) 'From moments to millennia. Theorizing scale and change in human history', in J. Robb and T. R. Pauketat (eds.) (2013b) *Big Histories, Human Lives. Tackling Problems of Scale in Archaeology*, 3–33, Santa Fe: School for Advanced Research Press.

Robb, J. and Pauketat, T. R. (eds.) (2013b) *Big Histories, Human Lives. Tackling Problems of Scale in Archaeology*, Santa Fe: School for Advanced Research Press.

Roscoe, P. (2009) 'Social signaling and the organization of small-scale society: the case of contact-era New Guinea', *Journal of Archaeological Method and Theory* 16(2): 69–116.

Rosenswig, R. M. and Cunningham, J. J. (2017a) 'Introducing modes of production in archaeology', in R. M. Rosenswig and J. J. Cunningham (2017b): 1–28.

Rosenswig, R. M. and Cunningham, J. J. (eds.) (2017b) *Modes of Production in Archaeology*, Gainesville: University Press of Florida.

Routledge, B., (2014) *Archaeology and State Theory. Subjects and Objects of Power*, London: Bloomsbury.

Routledge, B. (2021) 'Scaffolding and concept-metaphors: building archaeological knowledge and practice', in A. Killin and S. Allen-Hermanson (eds.), *Explorations in Archaeology and Philosophy*, 47–63, New York: Springer.

Rowlands, M. J. (1993) 'The role of memory in the transmission of culture', *World Archaeology* 25(2):141–51.

Rowlands, M. J., Larsen, M. and Kristiansen, K. (eds.) (1987) *Centre and Periphery in the Ancient World*, Cambridge: Cambridge University Press.

Sahlins, M. (1968) *Tribesmen*, Englewood Cliffs, NJ: Prentice-Hall.

Said, E. W. (1978) *Orientalism,* New York: Vintage Books.

Saitta, D. J. (1992) 'Radical archaeology and middle-range methodology', *Antiquity* 66: 886–97.

Saitta, D. J. (2007) *The Archaeology of Collective Action*, Gainesville: University Press of Florida.

Schmidt, R. A. and Voss, B. L. (eds.) (2000) *Archaeologies of Sexuality*, London: Routledge.

Scott, H. (2008) *The Essential Rosa Luxemburg*, Chicago, IL: Haymarket Books.

Service, E. R. (1962) *Primitive Social Organisation: An Evolutionary Perspective*, New York: Random House.

Service, E. R. (1967) 'Our contemporary ancestors: extant ages and extinct stages', in M. Fried, M. Harris and R. Murphy (eds.) *Warfare: The Anthropology of Armed Conflict and Aggression*, 160–7, Chicago, IL: American Museum of Natural History.

Schiffer, M. B. (1972) 'Archaeological context and systemic context', *American Antiquity* 37(2): 156–65.

Schiffer, M. B. (1976) *Behavioral Archeology*, New York: Academic Press.

Shanks, M. (2007) 'Symmetrical archaeology', *World Archaeology* 39(4): 589–96.

Shanks, M. and Tilley, C. (1987a) *Re-constructing Archaeology: Theory and Practice*, Cambridge: Cambridge University Press.

Shanks, M. and Tilley, C. (1987b) *Social Theory and Archaeology*, Cambridge: Plenum.

Shanks, M. and Tilley, C. (1989) 'Questions rather than Answers: Reply to Comments on Archaeology into the 1990s', *Norwegian Archaeological Review* 22(1): 42–53.

Shennan, S. (1993) 'Cultural transmission and cultural change', in S. van der Leeuw and R. Torrence (eds.) *What's New: A Closer Look at the Process of Innovation*, 330–46, London: Unwin Hyman.

Shennan, S. (2002) *Genes, Memes and Human History. Darwinian Archaeology and Cultural Evolution*, London: Thames and Hudson.

Shennan, S. (2012) 'Darwinian cultural evolution', in I. Hodder (ed.) *Archaeological Theory Today*, Second edition, 15–36, Cambridge: Polity Press.

Shennan, S. (2018) *The First Farmers of Europe. An Evolutionary Perspective*, Cambridge: Cambridge University Press.

Sherratt, A. and Sherratt, S. (1993) 'The growth of the Mediterranean in the early first millennium B.C.', *World Archaeology* 24: 361–78.

Shilling, C. (2012) *The Body and Social Theory*, Third edition, London: Sage.

Silliman, S. W. (ed.) (2008) *Collaborating at the Trowel's Edge*, Tucson: University of Arizona Press.

Silliman, S. W. (2016) 'Disentangling the archaeology of colonialism and indigeneity', in L. Der and F. Fernandini (eds.), *Archaeology of Entanglement*, 31–49, Abingdon: Routledge.

Sokal, A. and Bricmont, J. (1998) *Intellectual Impostures*, London: Profile Books.

Spriggs, M. (ed.) (1984) *Marxist Perspectives in Archaeology*, Cambridge: Cambridge University Press.

Spriggs, M. (2008) 'Ethnographic parallels and the denial of history', *World Archaeology* 40: 538–52.

Ste-Croix, G.E.M. de (1981) *The Class Struggle in the Ancient Greek World from the Archaic Age to the Arab Conquests*, London: Duckworth.

Steel, L. (2013) *Materiality and Consumption in the Bronze Age Mediterranean*, Abingdon: Routledge.

Steward, J. H. (1955) *Theory of Culture Change: The Theory of Multilinear Evolution*, Urbana: University of Illinois Press.

Therborn, G. (2010) *From Marxism to Post-Marxism?* London: Verso.

Thomas, J. (1996) *Time, Culture and Identity. An Interpretive Archaeology*, London: Routledge.

Thomas, J. (ed.) (2000) *Interpretive Archaeology*, London: Leicester University Press.

Thomas, J. (2004) *Archaeology and Modernity*, Abingdon: Routledge.

Thomas, J. (2007) 'The trouble with material culture', *Journal of Iberian Archaeology* 9(10): 11–23.

Thomas, J. (2015) 'The future of archaeological theory', *Antiquity* 89: 1287–96.

Thomas, N. (1991) *Entangled objects. Exchange, Material Culture and Colonialism in the Pacific*, Cambridge, MA: Harvard University Press.

Tilley, C. (1994) *A Phenomenology of Landscape*, Oxford: Berg.

Tilley, C. (2004) *The Materiality of Stone. Explorations of Landscape Phenomenology*, Oxford: Berg.

Tilley, C., Keane, W., Kuchler, S., Rowlands, M. and Spyer, P. (eds.) (2006) *Handbook of Material Culture*, London: Sage Publications.

Tosi, M. (1984) 'The notion of craft specialization and its representation in the archaeological record of early states in the Turanian Basin', in M. Spriggs (ed.) *Marxist Perspectives in Archaeology*, 22–52, Cambridge: Cambridge University Press.

Toulmin, S. E. (1958) *The Uses of Argument*, Cambridge: Cambridge University Press.

Treherne, P. (1995) 'The warrior's beauty: the masculine body and self-identity in Bronze Age Europe', *Journal of European Archaeology* 3(1): 105–44.

Trentmann, F. (2009) 'Materiality in the future of history: things, practices and politics', *Journal of British Studies* 48: 283–307.

Trigger, B. G. (1980a) *Gordon Childe. Revolutions in Archaeology*, London: Thames and Hudson.

Trigger, B. G. (1980b) 'Archaeology and the image of the American Indian', *American Antiquity* 45: 662–76.

Trigger, B. G. (1984) 'Alternative archaeologies: nationalist, colonialist, imperialist', *Man* 19: 355–70.

Trigger, B. G. (1993) 'Marxism in contemporary Western archaeology', *Archaeological Method and Theory* 5: 159–200.

Trigger, B. G. (1998) *Sociocultural Evolution*, Oxford: Blackwell Publishers.

Trigger, B. G. (2006) *A History of Archaeological Thought.* (Second edition), Cambridge: Cambridge University Press.

Urban, P. A. and Schortman, E. (2019) *Archaeological Theory in Practice.* (Second edition), New York: Routledge.

Van Dyke, R. M. (2011) 'Imagined pasts reimagined. Memory and Ideology in Archaeology', in R. Bernbeck and R. H. McGuire (eds.), *Ideologies in Archaeology*, 233–53, Tucson: University of Arizona Press.

Van Dyke, R. M. (2020) 'Chaco Gathers. Experience and assemblage in the ancient Southwest', in S. M. Alt and T. R. Pauketat (eds.) *New Materialisms Ancient Urbanisms*, 40–64, Abingdon: Routledge.

Van Dyke, R. M. (2021) 'Ethics, not objects', *Cambridge Archaeological Journal* 31(3): 487–93.

Van Dyke, R. M. and Alcock, S. E. (eds.) (2003) *Archaeologies of Memory*, Oxford: Blackwell.

Voss, B.L. (2008) 'Sexuality Studies in Archaeology', *Annual Review of Anthropology* 37(1): 317–36.

Wallerstein, I. (1974) *The Modern World-System: Capitalist Agriculture and the Origins of European World-Economy in the Sixteenth Century*. New York: Academic Press.

Watts, C. (ed.) (2013a) *Relational Archaeologies. Humans, Animals, Things*, Abingdon: Routledge.

Watts, C. (2013b) 'Relational archaeologies: roots and routes', in C. Watts (ed.) *Relational Archaeologies. Humans, Animals, Things*, 1–20, Abingdon: Routledge.

White, L. A. (1959) *The Evolution of Culture*, New York: McGraw Hill.

Williams, H. (ed.) (2003) *Archaeologies of Remembering. Death and Memory in Past Societies*, London: Plenum.

Winterhalder, B. and Smith, E. A. (eds.) (1981) *Hunter-Gatherer Foraging Strategies: Ethnographic and Archaeological Analyses*, Chicago, IL: Chicago University Press.

Witmore, C. (2007) 'Symmetrical archaeology: excerpts from a manifesto', *World Archaeology* 39(4): 546–62.

Woodward, A. and Hughes, G. (2007) 'Deposits and doorways: patterns within the Iron Age settlement at Crick Covert Farm, Northamptonshire', in C. Haselgrove and R. Pope (eds.) *The Earlier Iron Age in Britain and the near Continent*, 185–203, Oxford: Oxbow Books.

Wright, R. P. (1991) 'Women's labour and pottery production in prehistory', in J. M. Gero and M. W. Conkey (eds.) *Engendering Archaeology. Women and Prehistory*, 194–223, Oxford: Blackwell.

Wurst, L. (1991) 'Employees must be of moral and temperate habits": rural and urban elite ideologies', in R. Paynter and R. H. McGuire (eds.) *The Archaeology of Inequality*, 125–49, Oxford: Blackwell

Wylie, A. (1991) 'Gender theory and the archaeological record: why is there no archaeology of gender?'. In J. M. Gero and M. W. Conkey (eds.) *Engendering Archaeology. Women and Prehistory*, 31–54, Oxford: Blackwell.

Wylie, A. (2002) *Thinking from Things. Essays in the Philosophy of Archaeology*, Berkeley: University of California Press.

Zahavi, D. (2019) *Phenomenology. The Basics*, Abingdon: Routledge.

INDEX